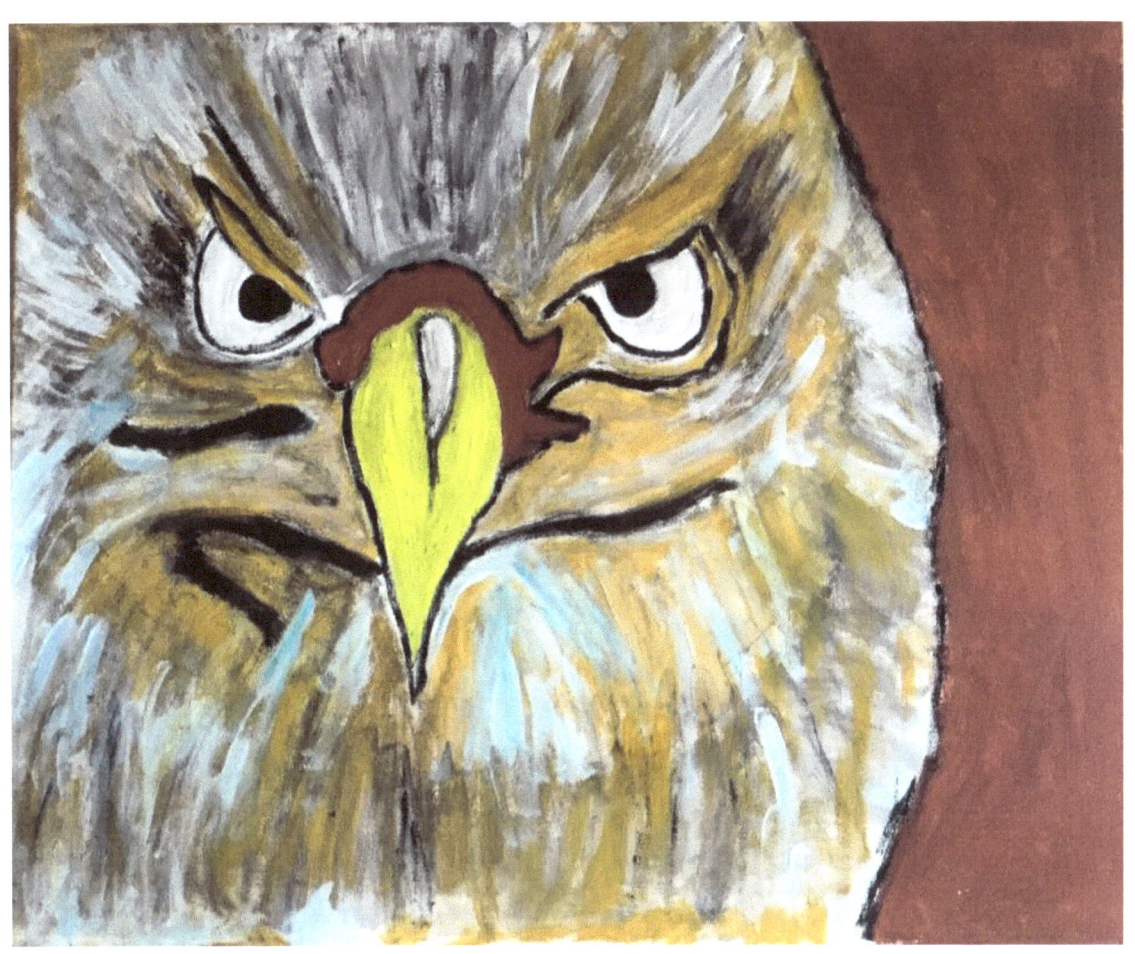

„Hawk" (Oil on canvas)

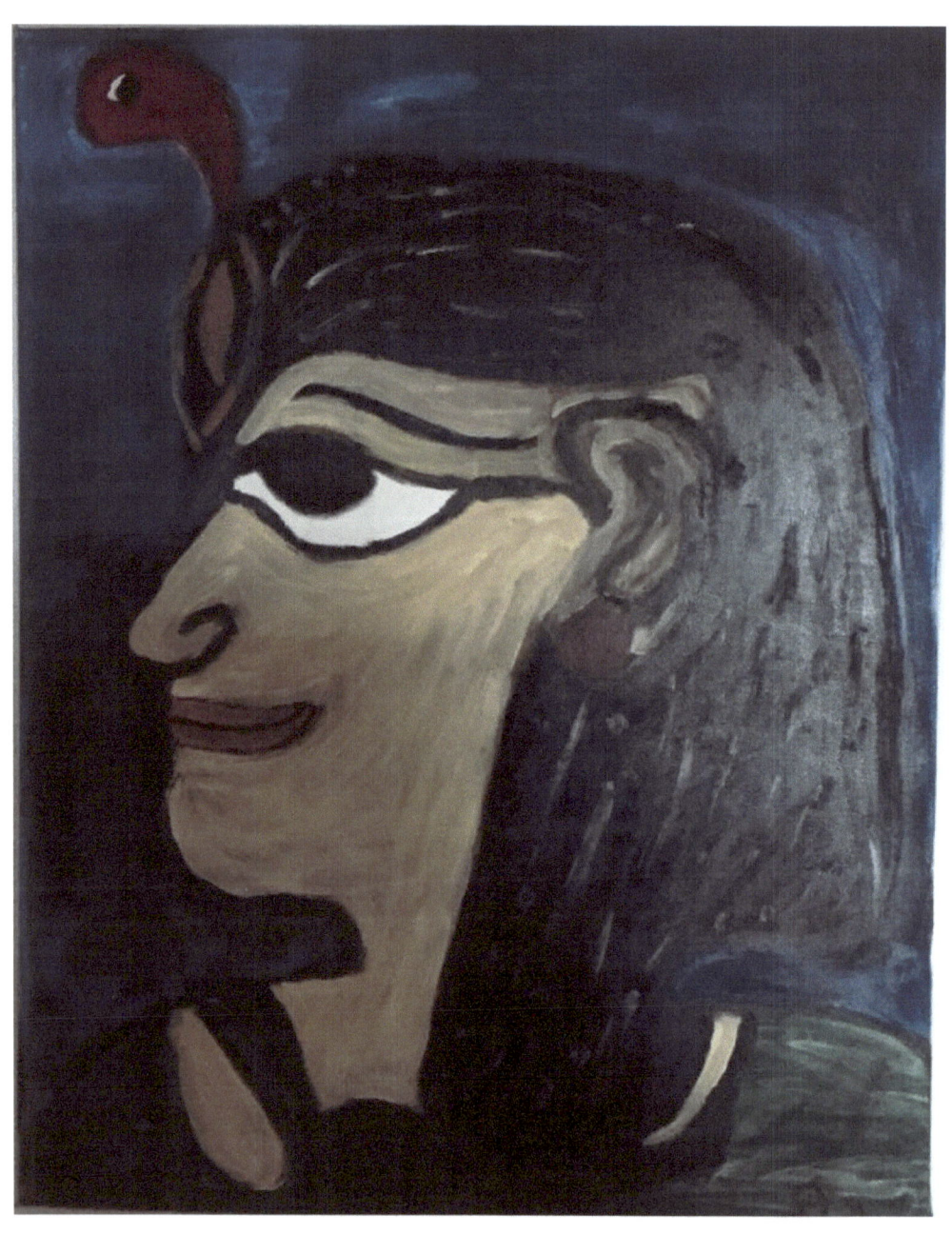

„Pharao" (Oil on canvas)

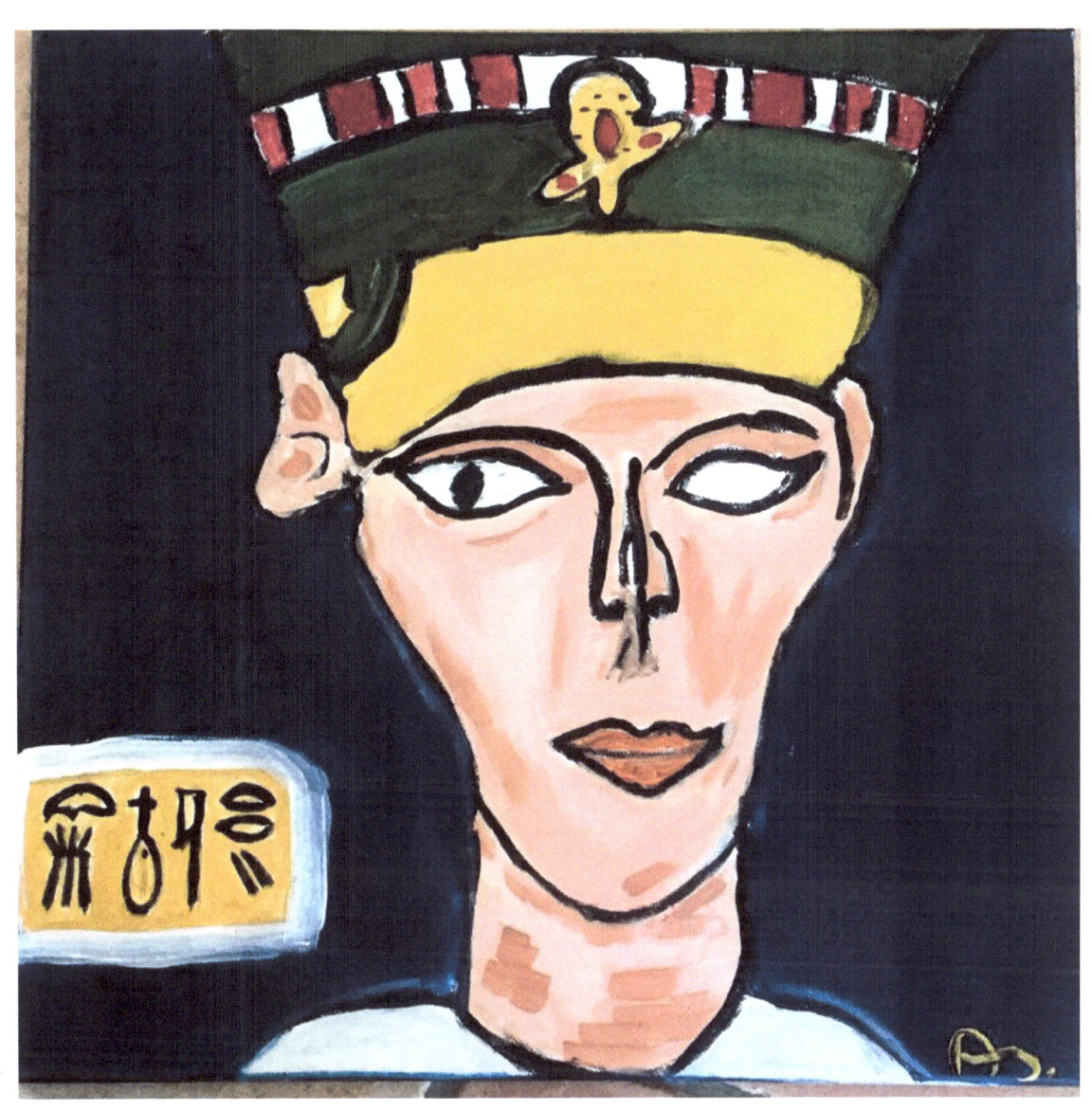

Nifrititi (Acryl on canvas)

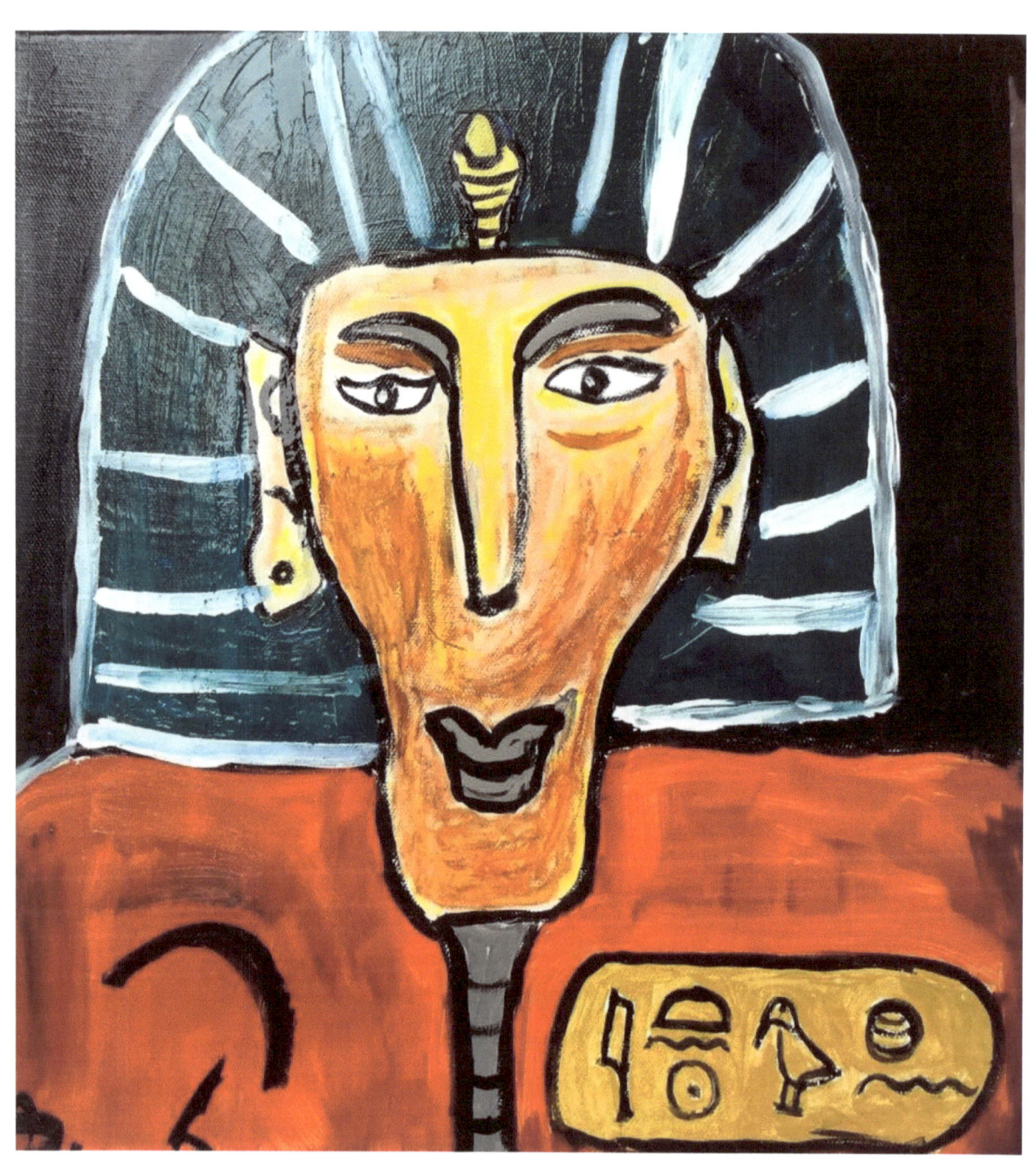

Akhenaten Acryl on canvas)

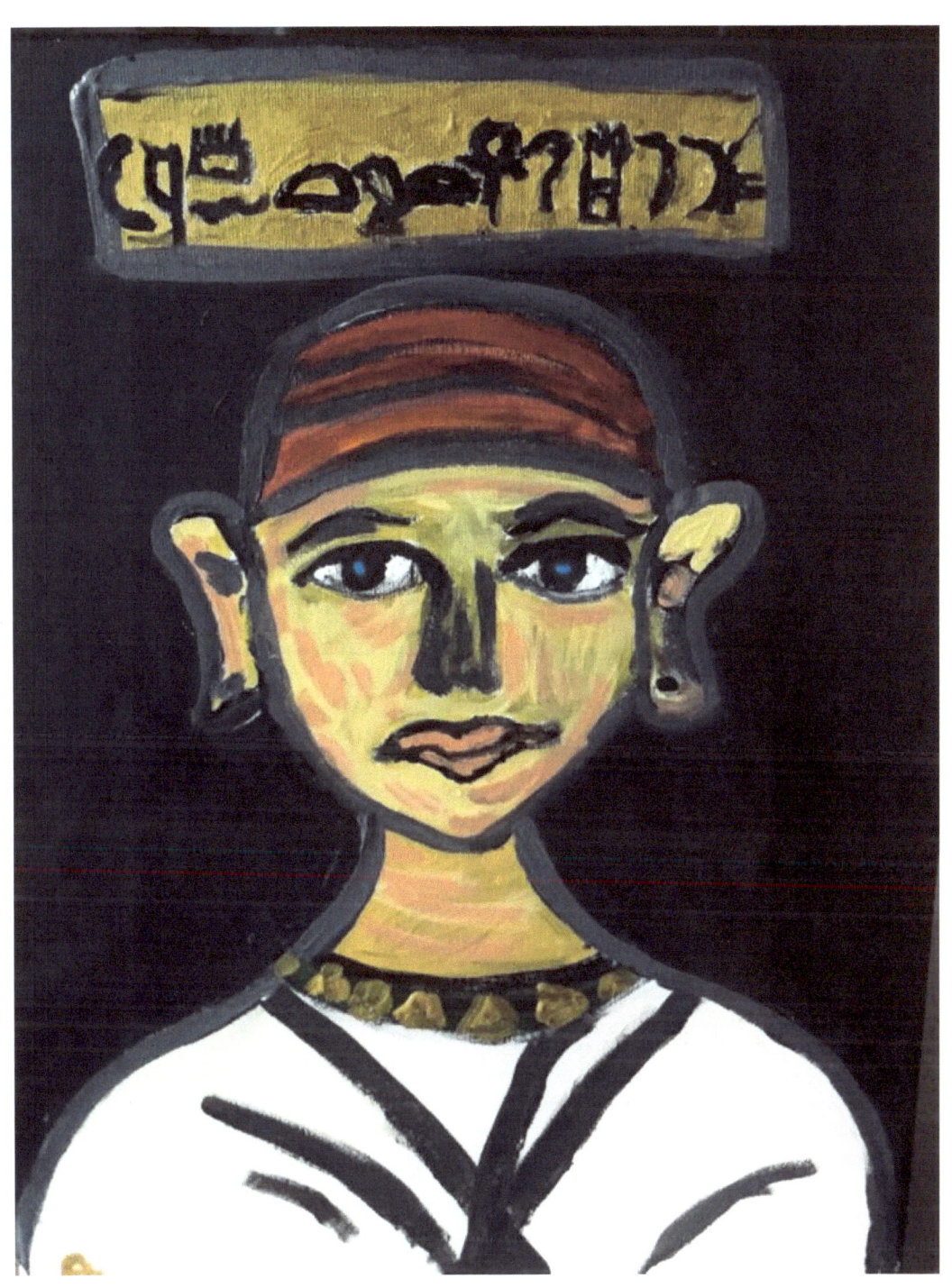

„Tut" (Acryl on canvas)

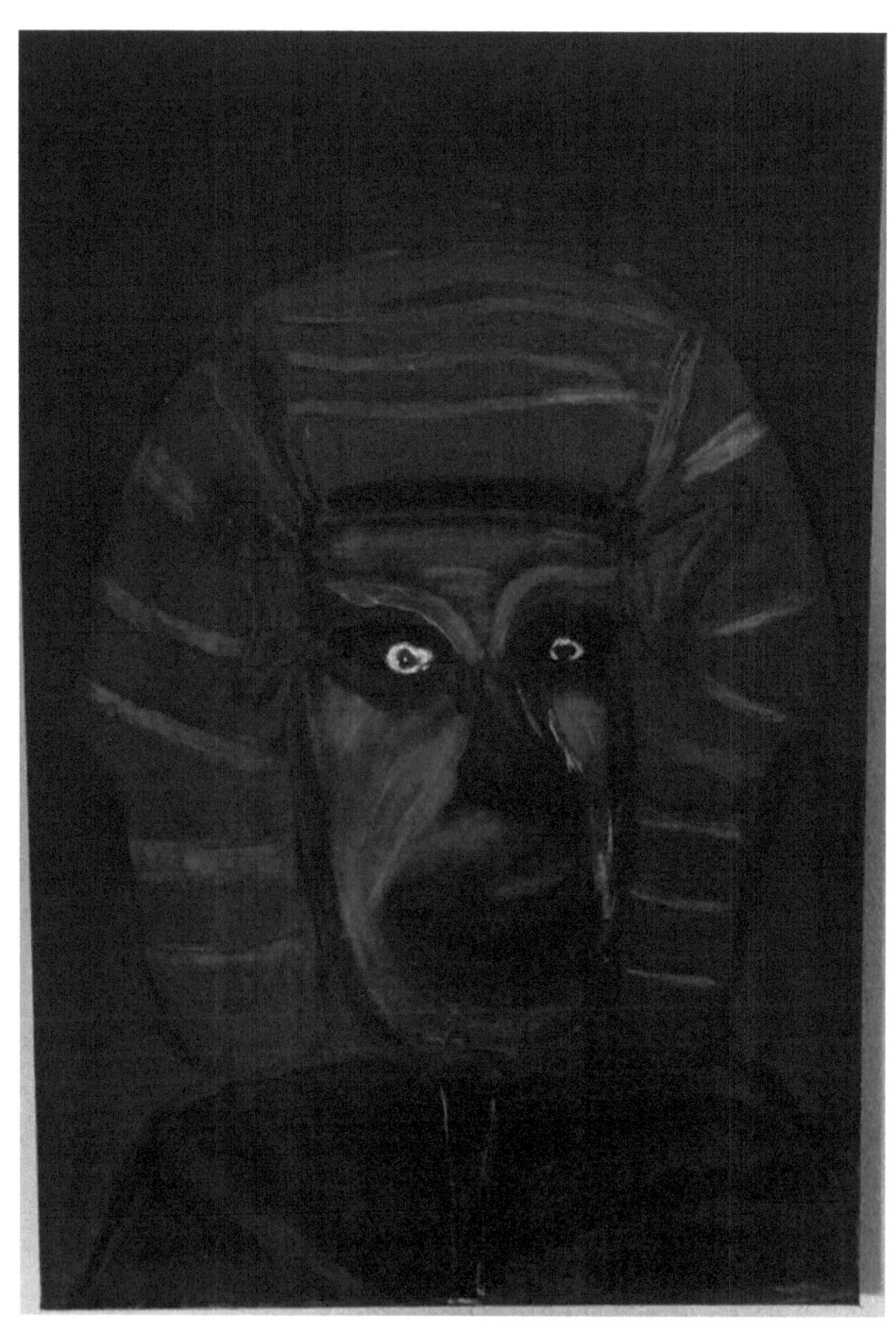

„Paul" (Acryl on canvas)

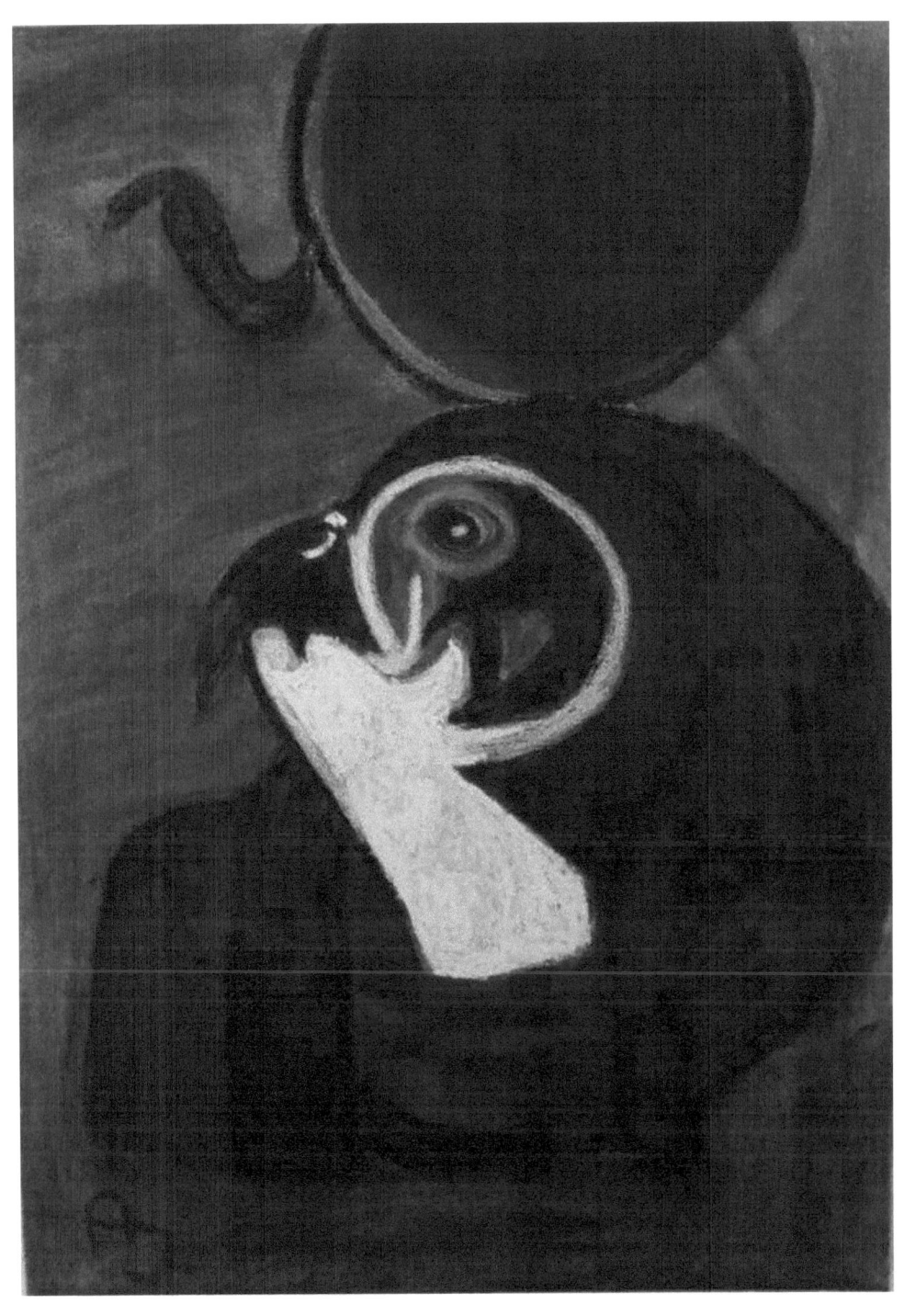

„Horus" (Mixed on canvas)

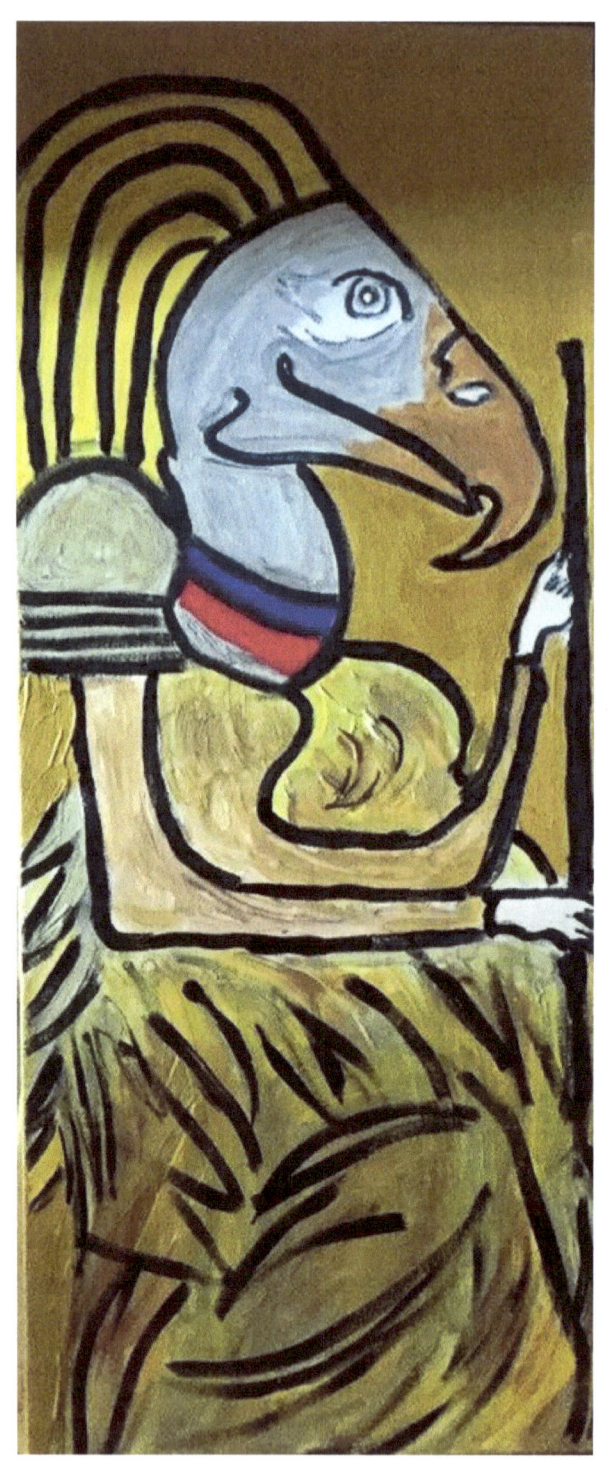

„Tahuti" (Acryl on canvas)

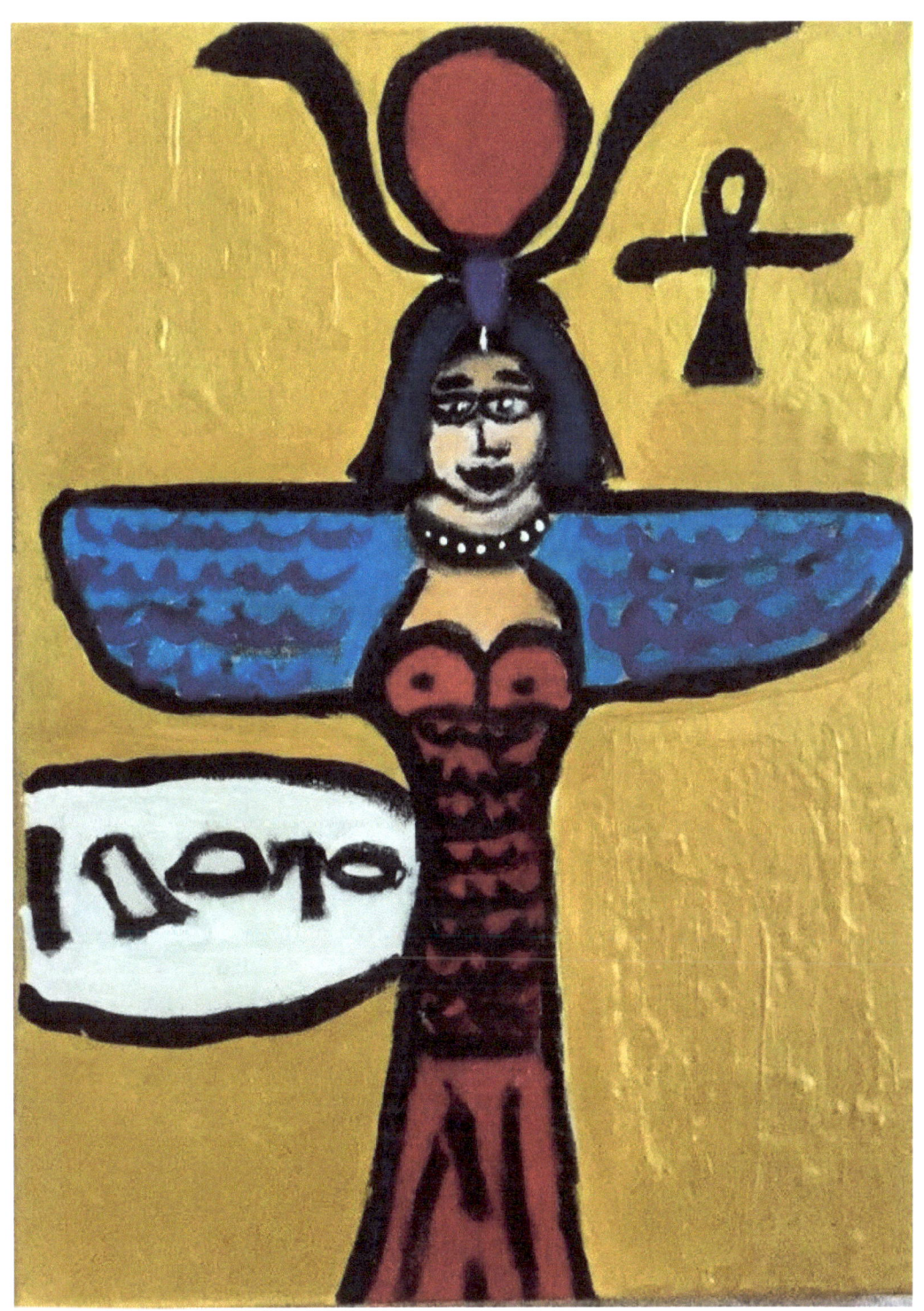

„Bibi Goddess" (Acryl on canvas)

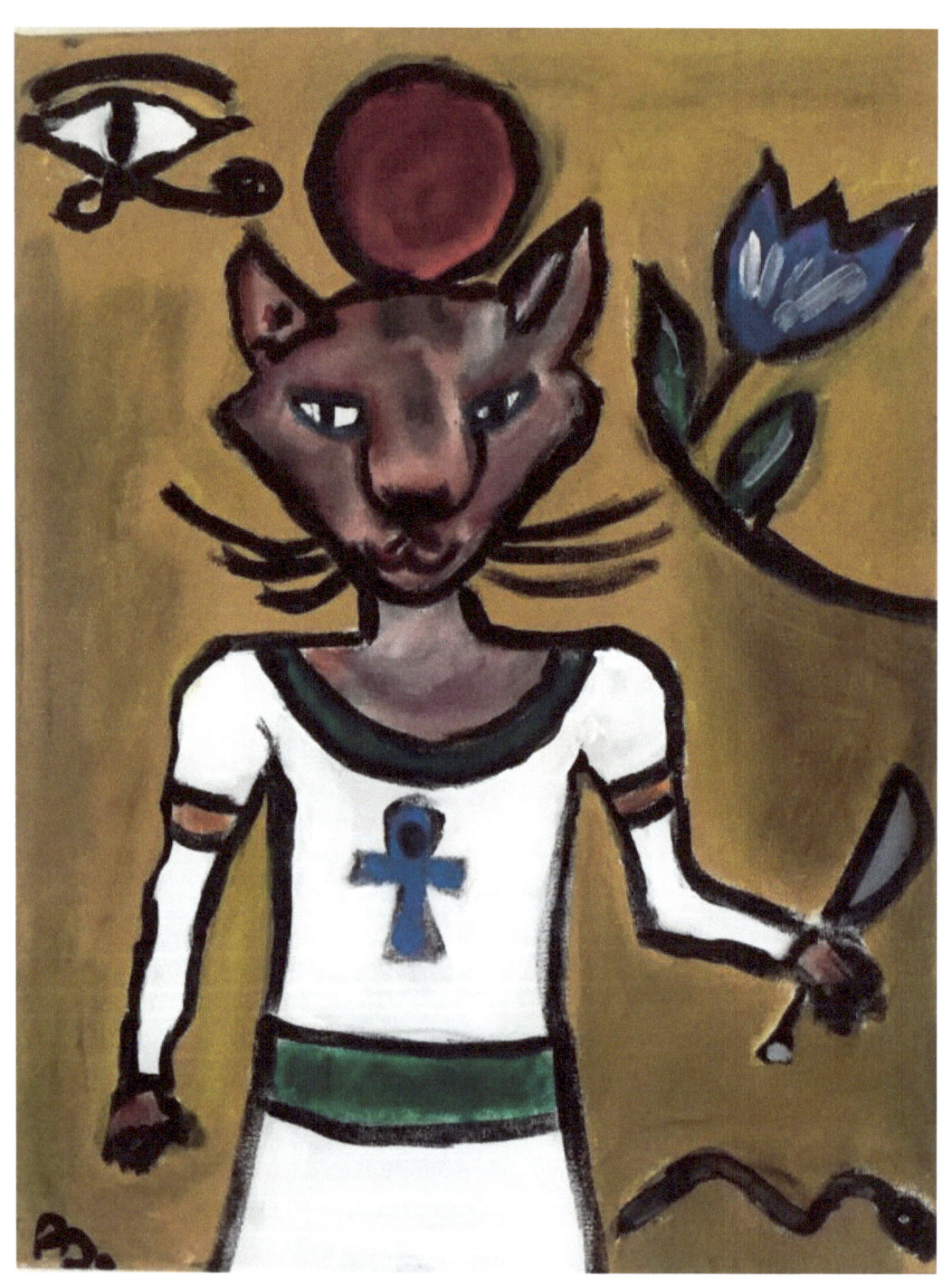

„Bastet" (Acryl on canvas)

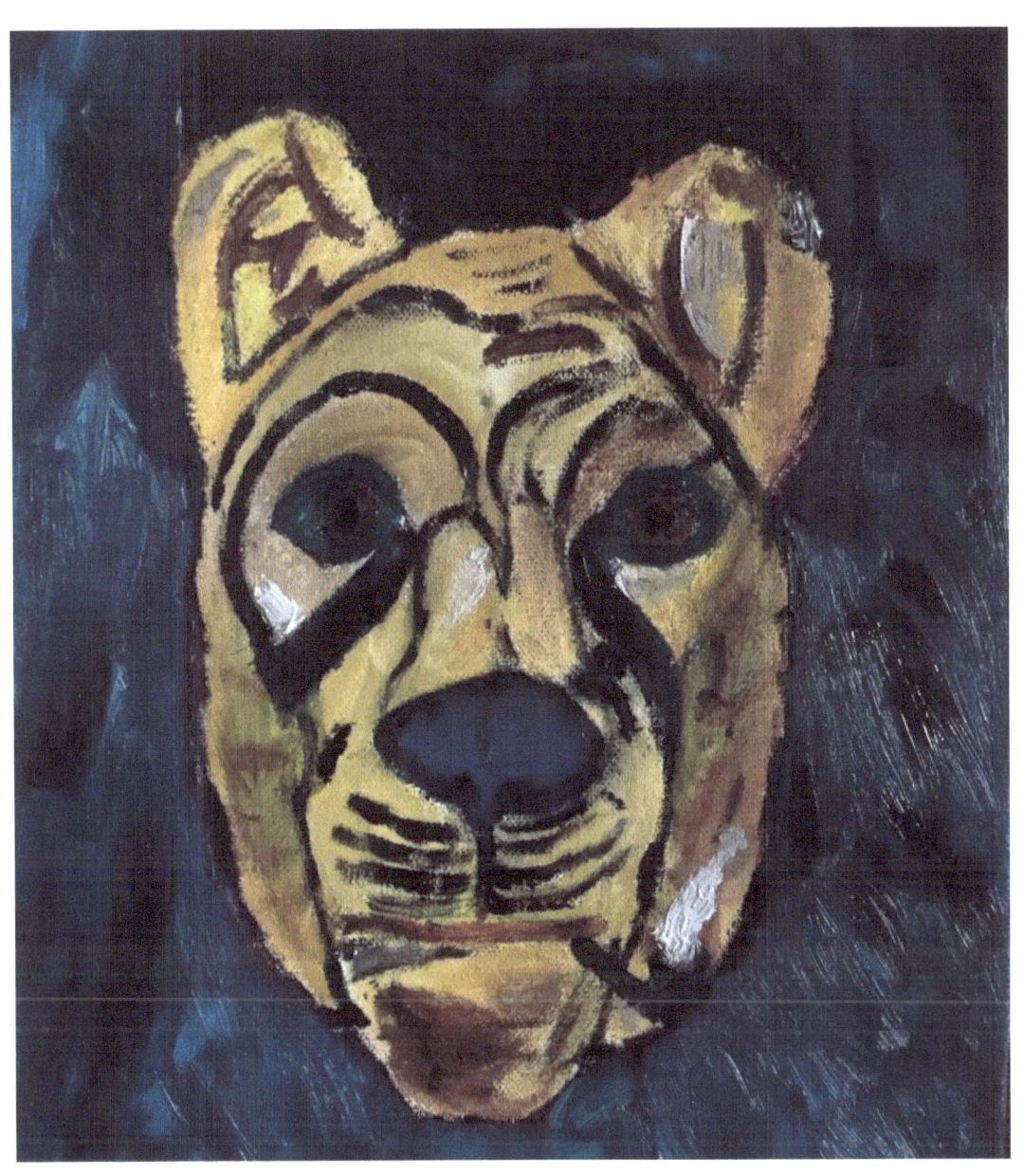

„Lion with pipe" (Mixed on canvas)

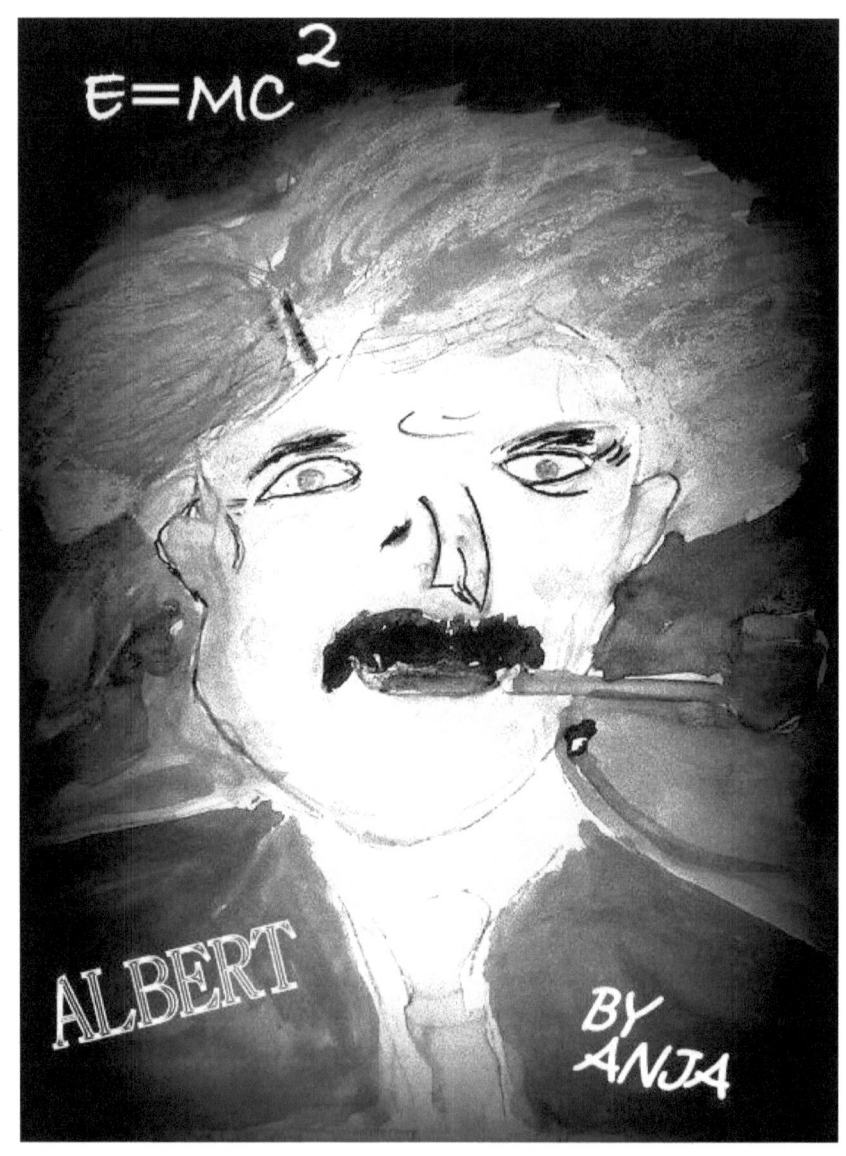

„Albert by Anja" (Charcoal on paper)

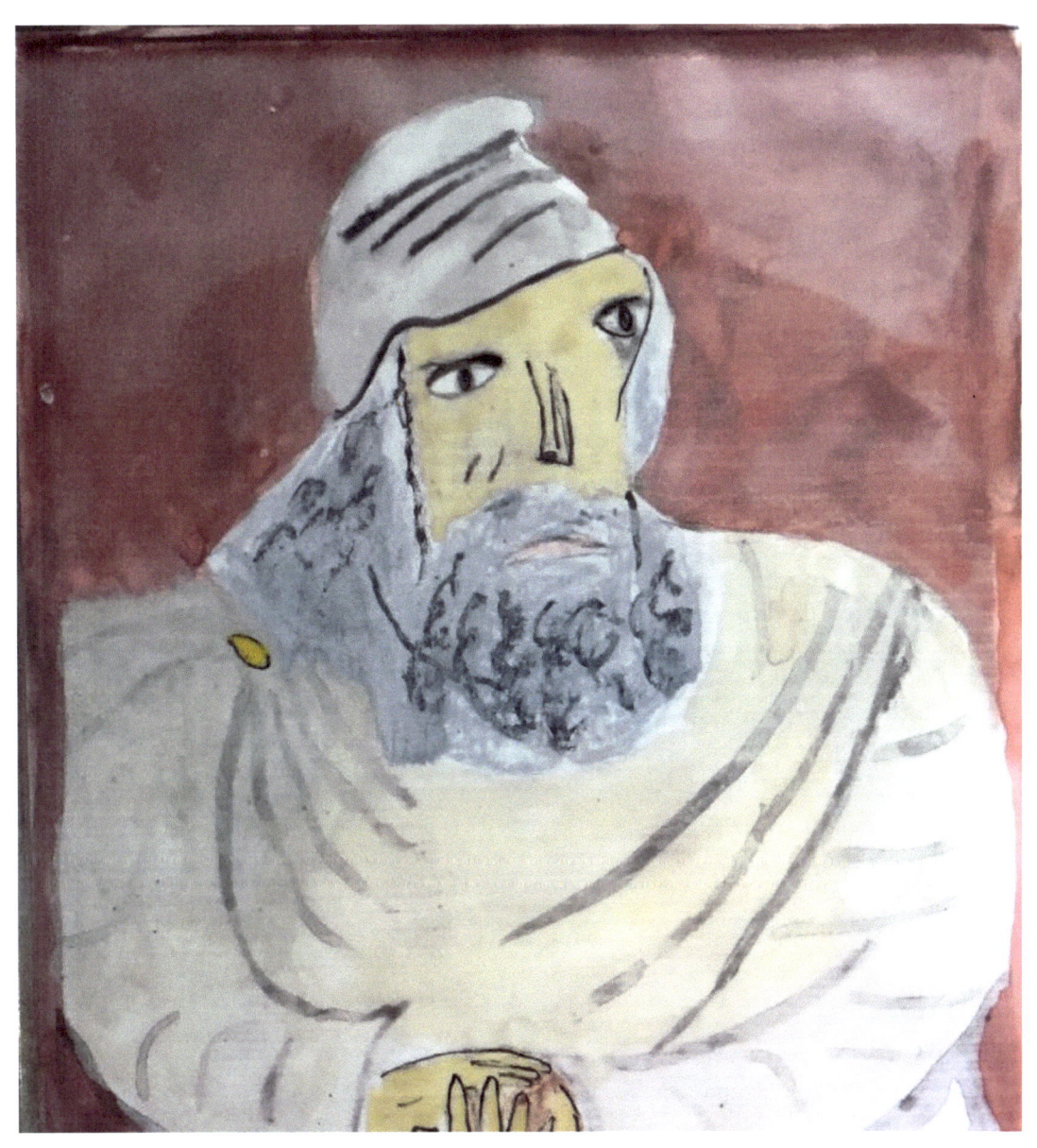

„Pythagoras" (Aquarell)

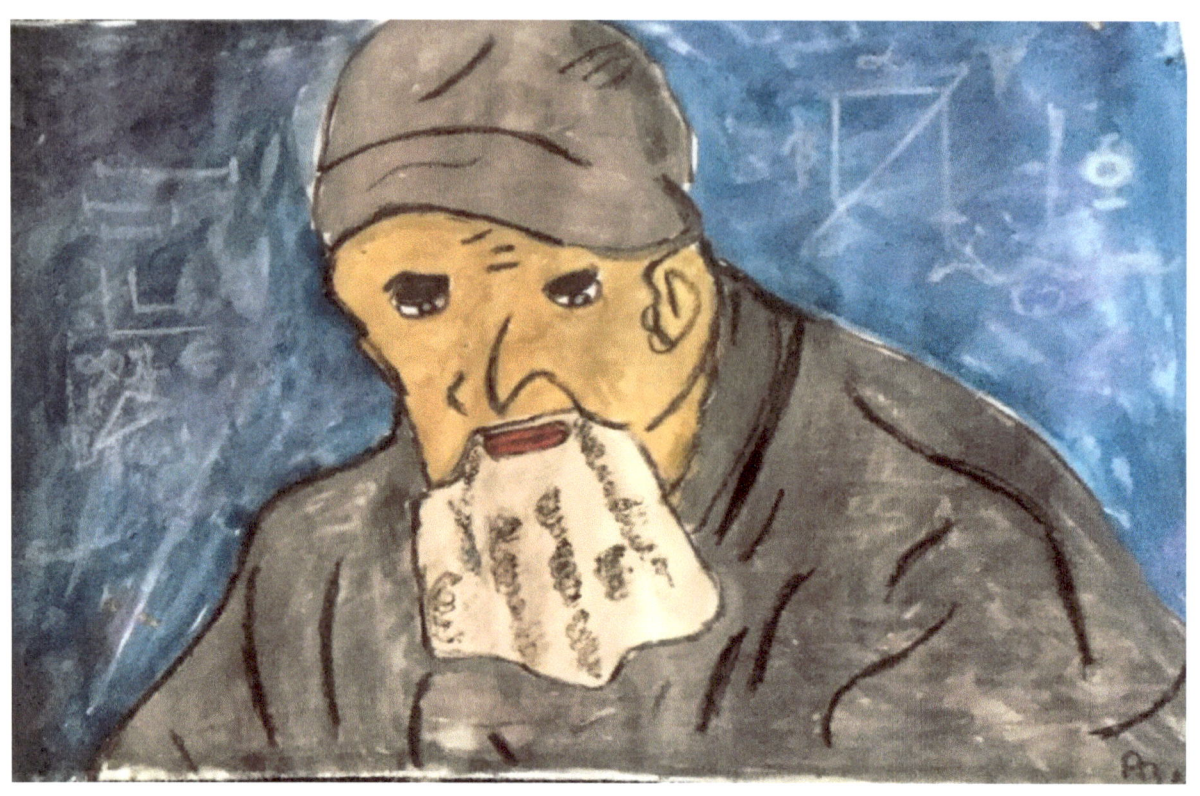

„Archimedes" (Aquarell)

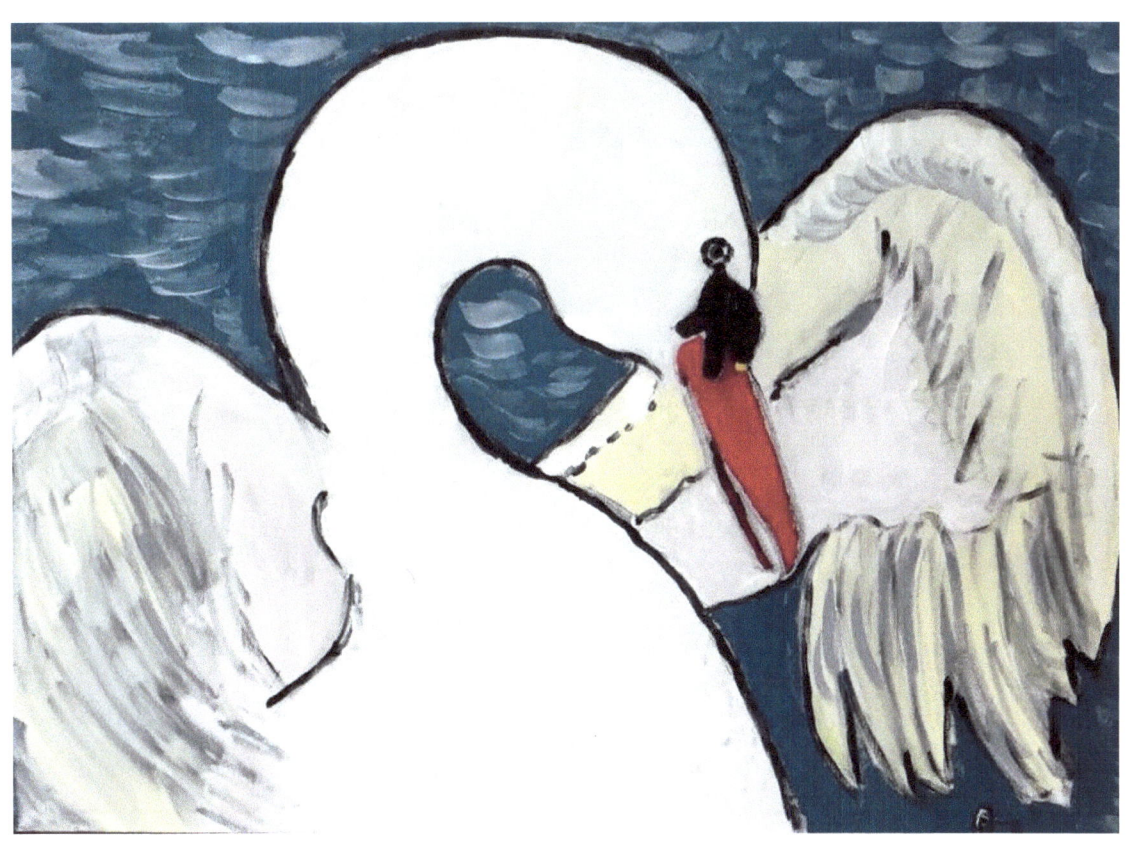

„Swan" (Acryl on canvas)

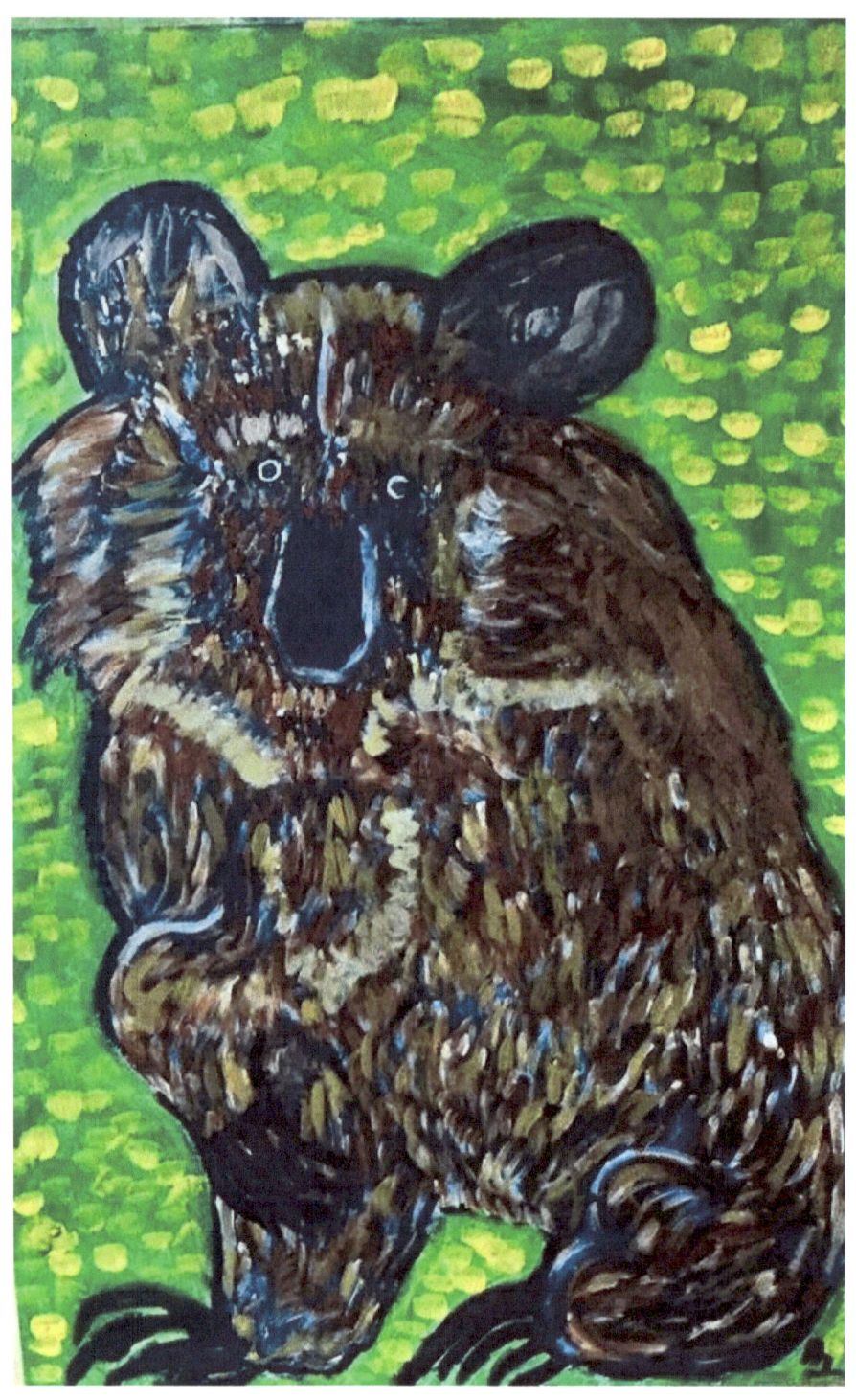

„Bruno the problem bear" (Acryl on canvas)

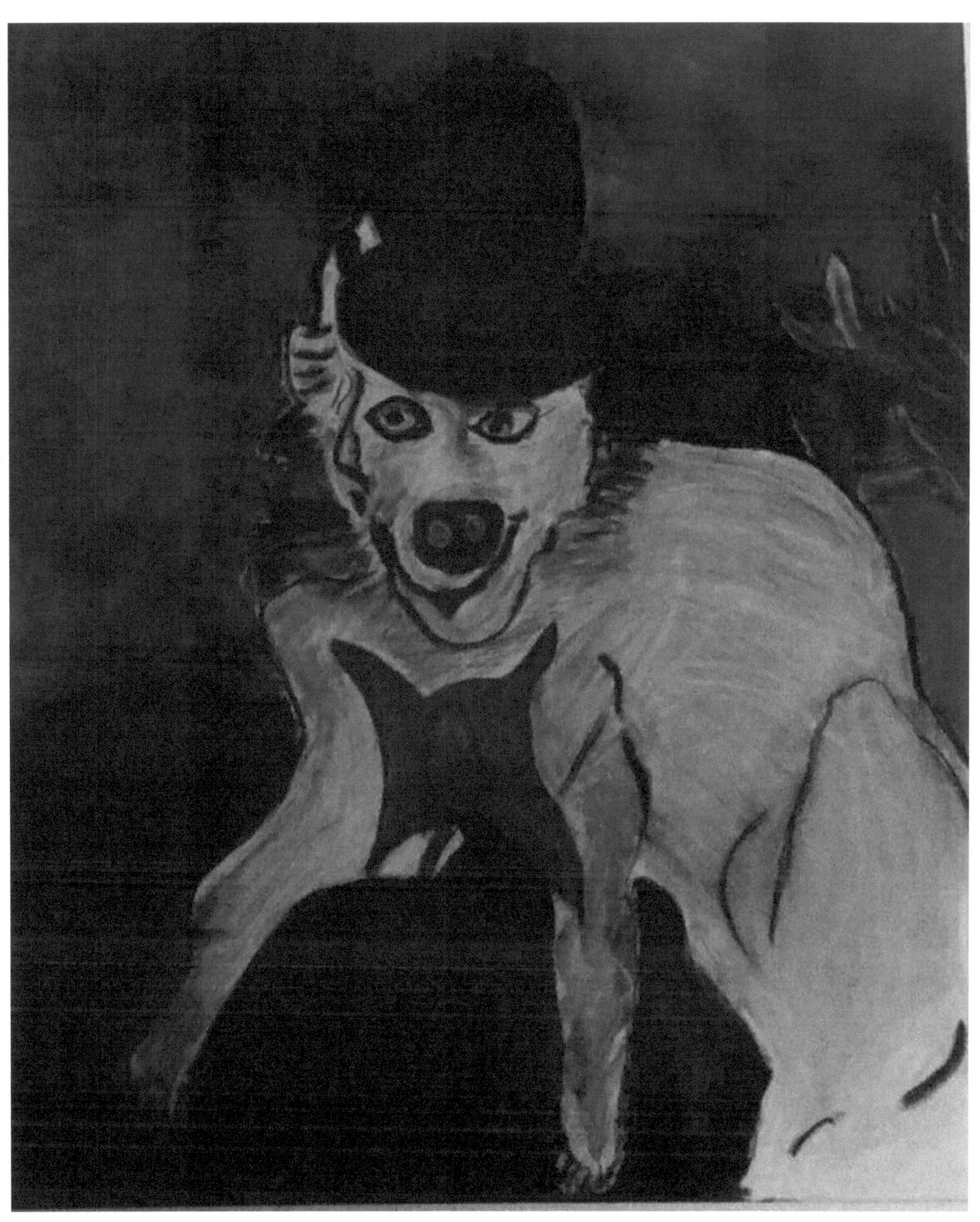

„Loup" (Acryl on canvas)

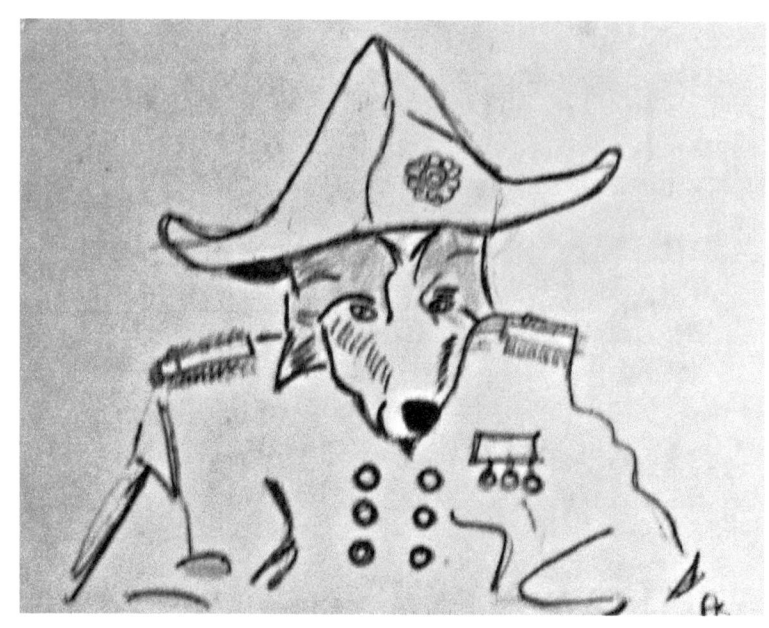

„Amarok General" (Charcoal on paper)

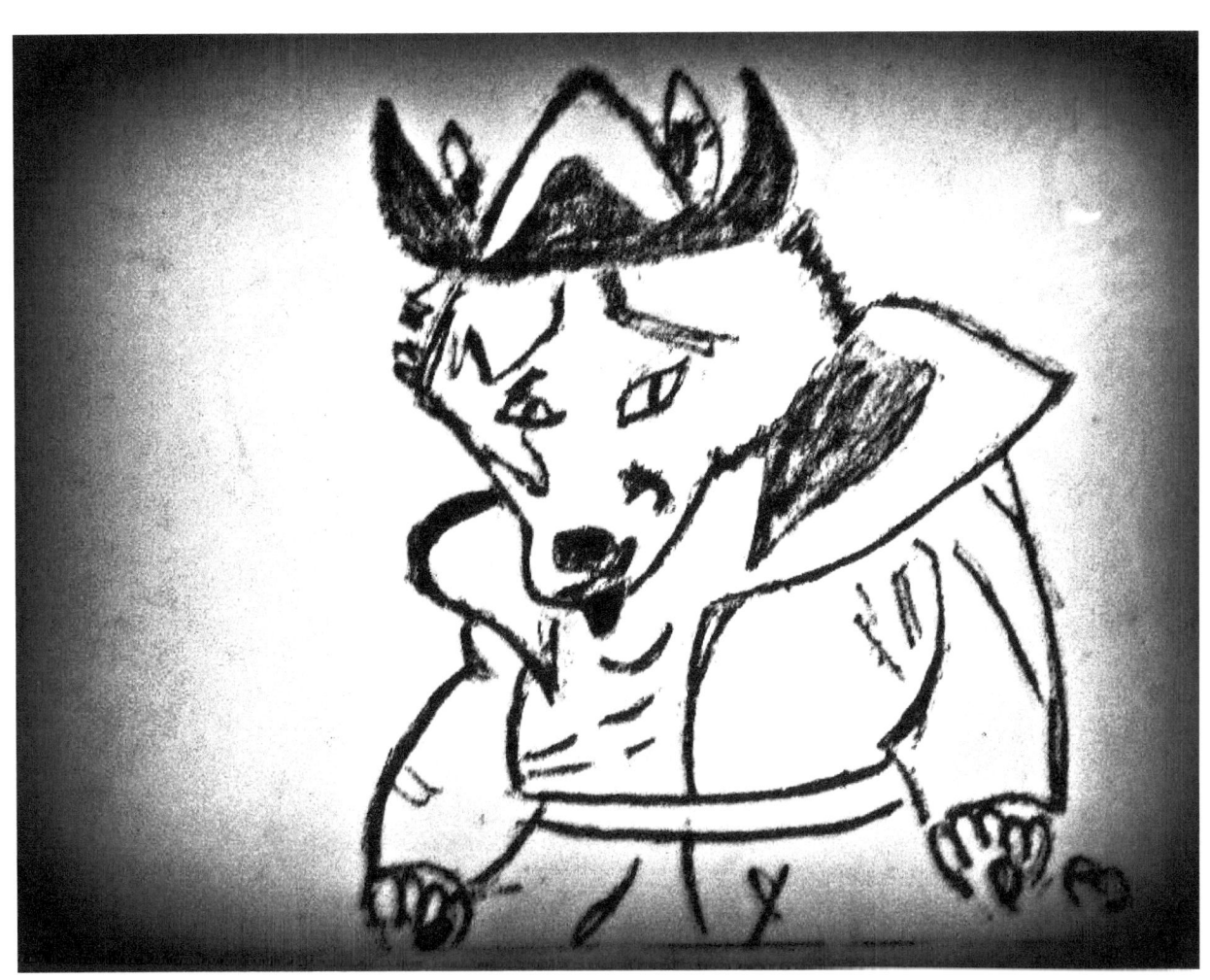

„Billy the blind" (Charcoal on paper)

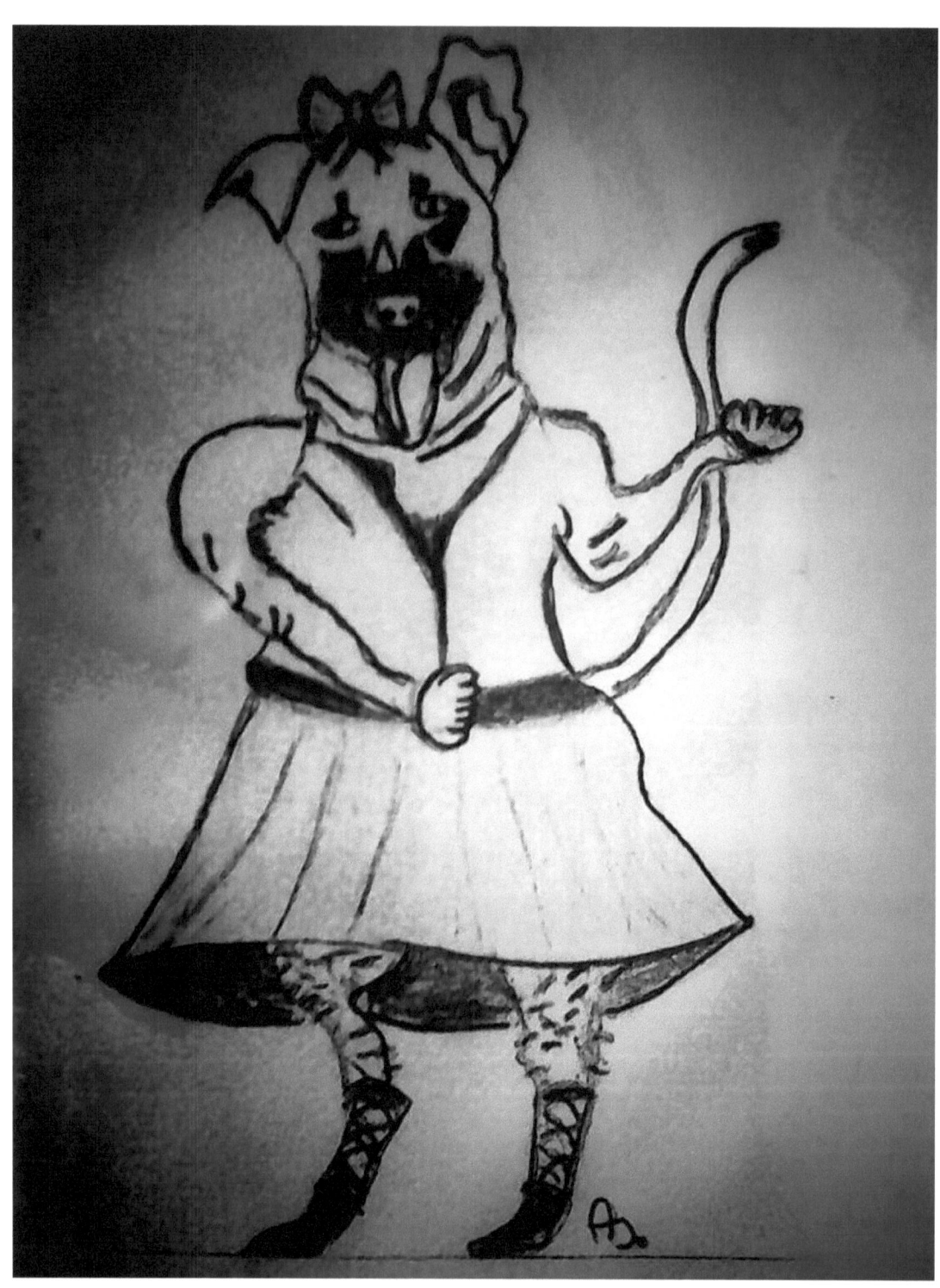

„Baby la Danseuse" (Charcoal on paper)

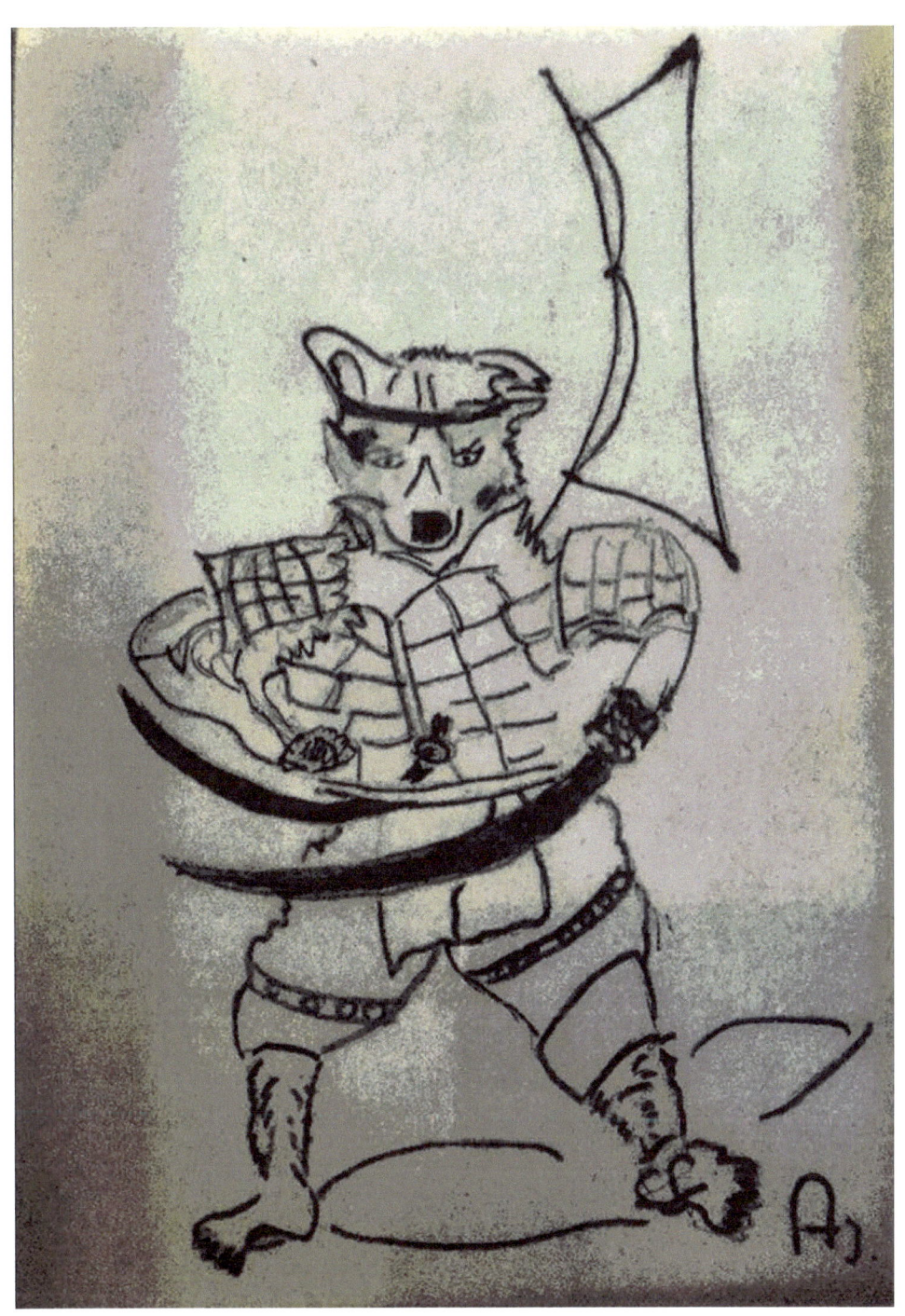

„Huyabusa San" (Charcoal on paper)

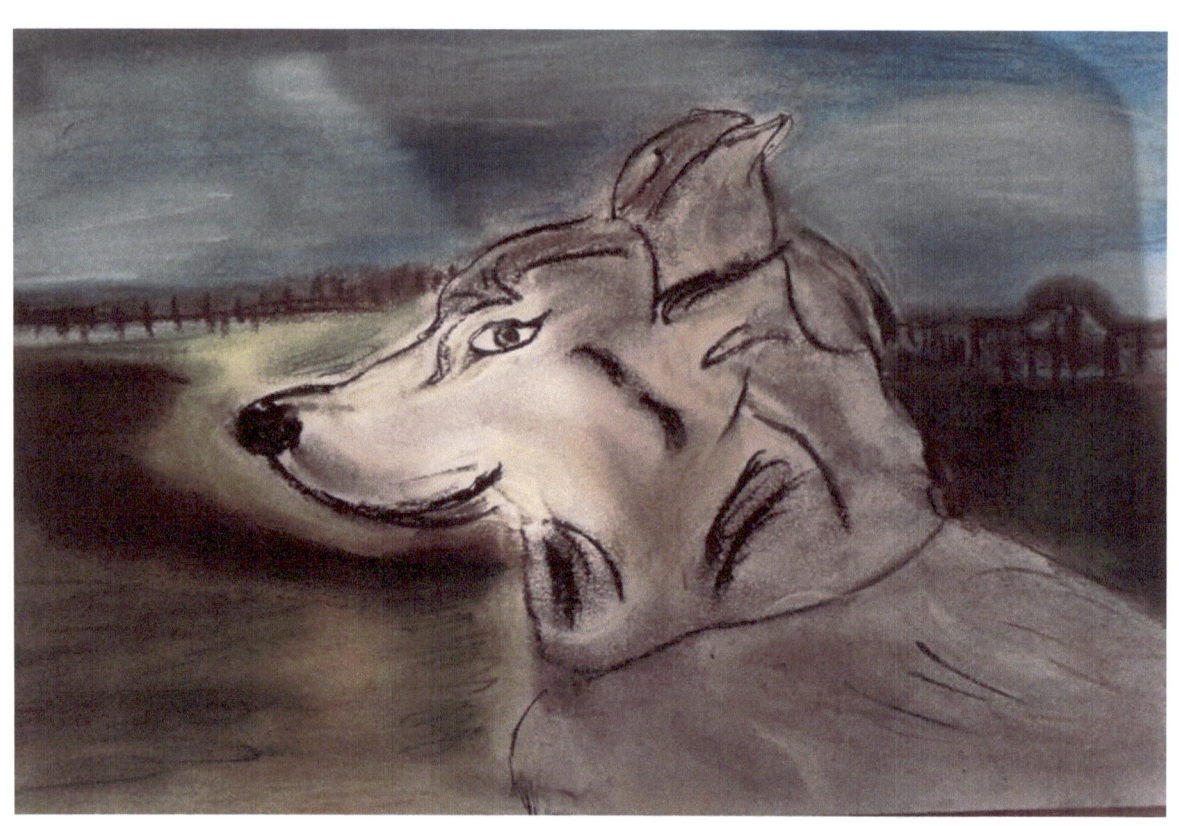

„Toulouse" (Crayon on paper)

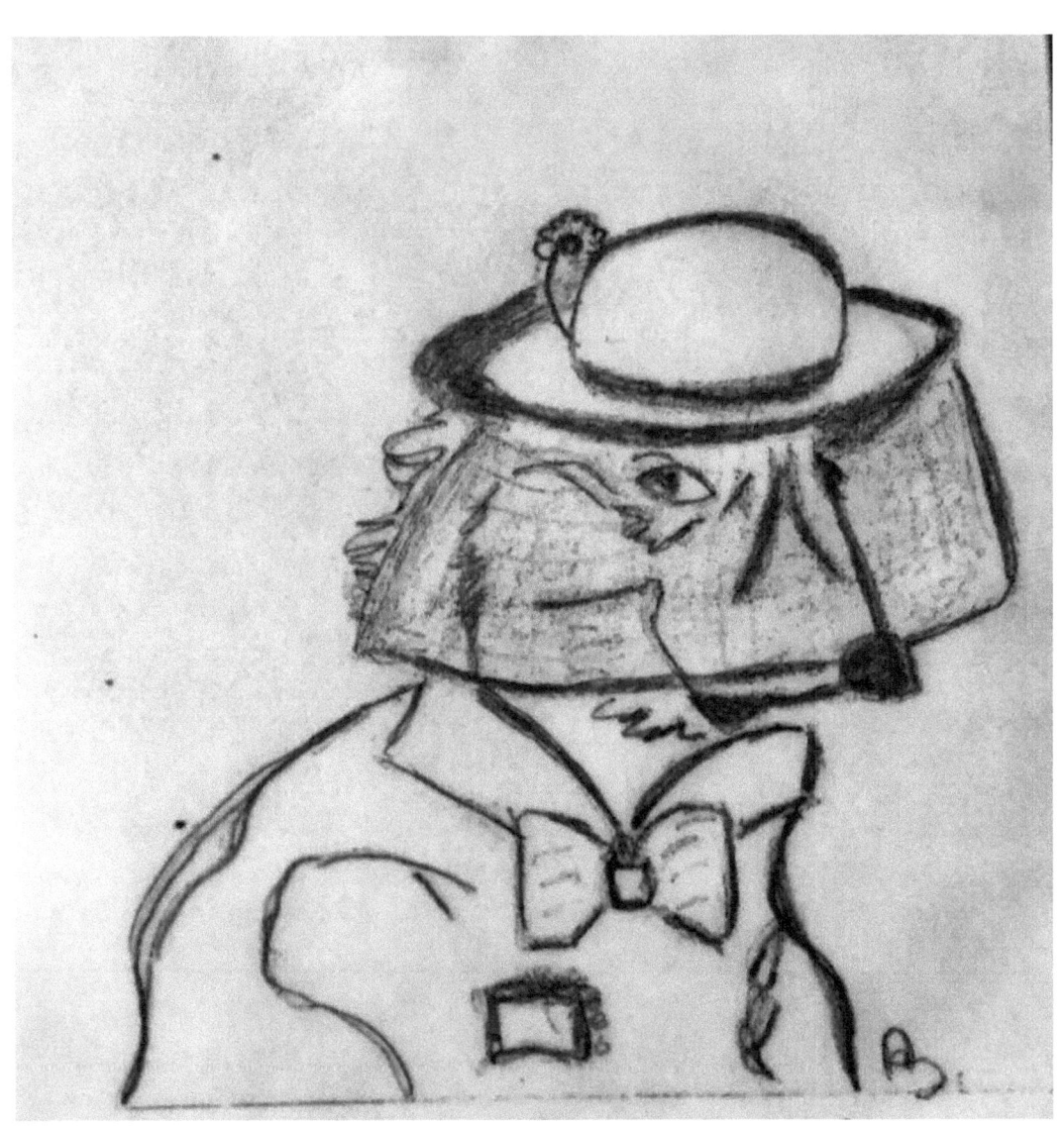

„Gixy" (Charcoal on paper)

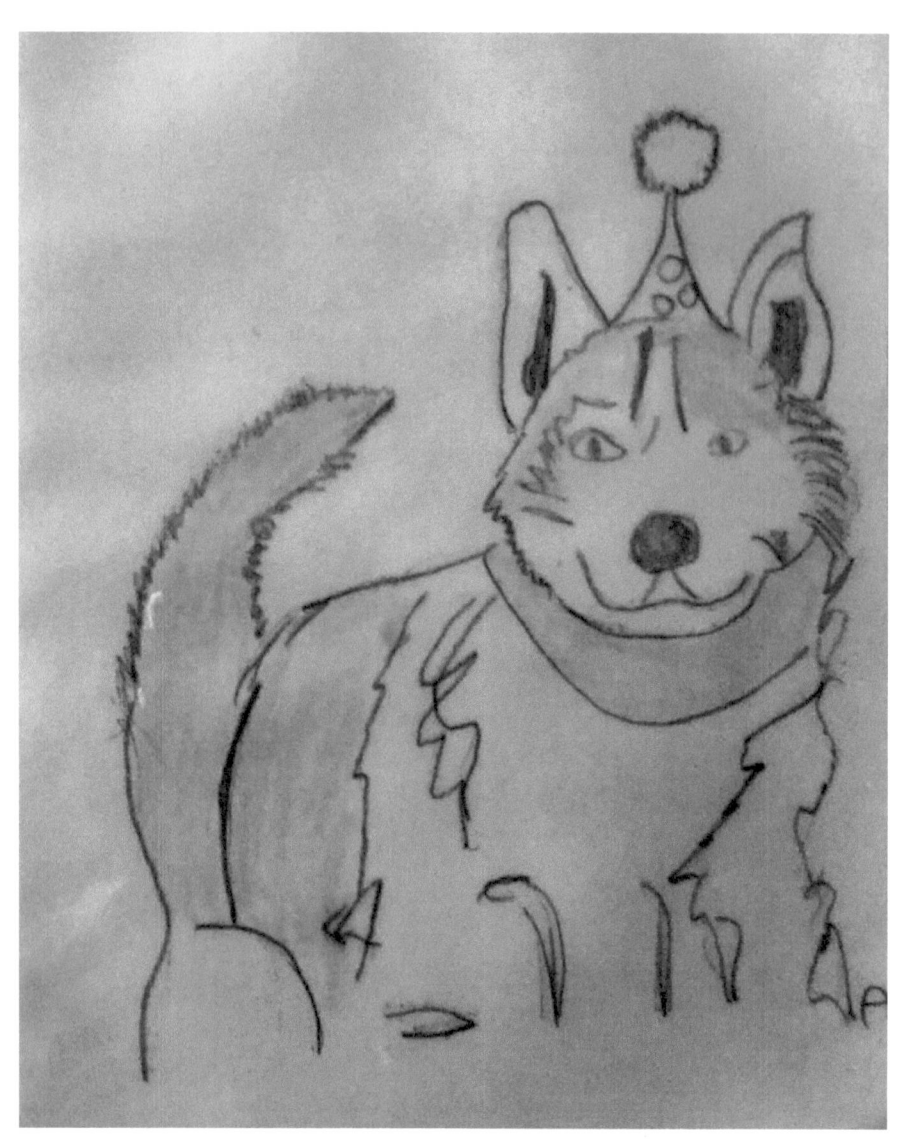

„Trapper" (Mixed on paper)

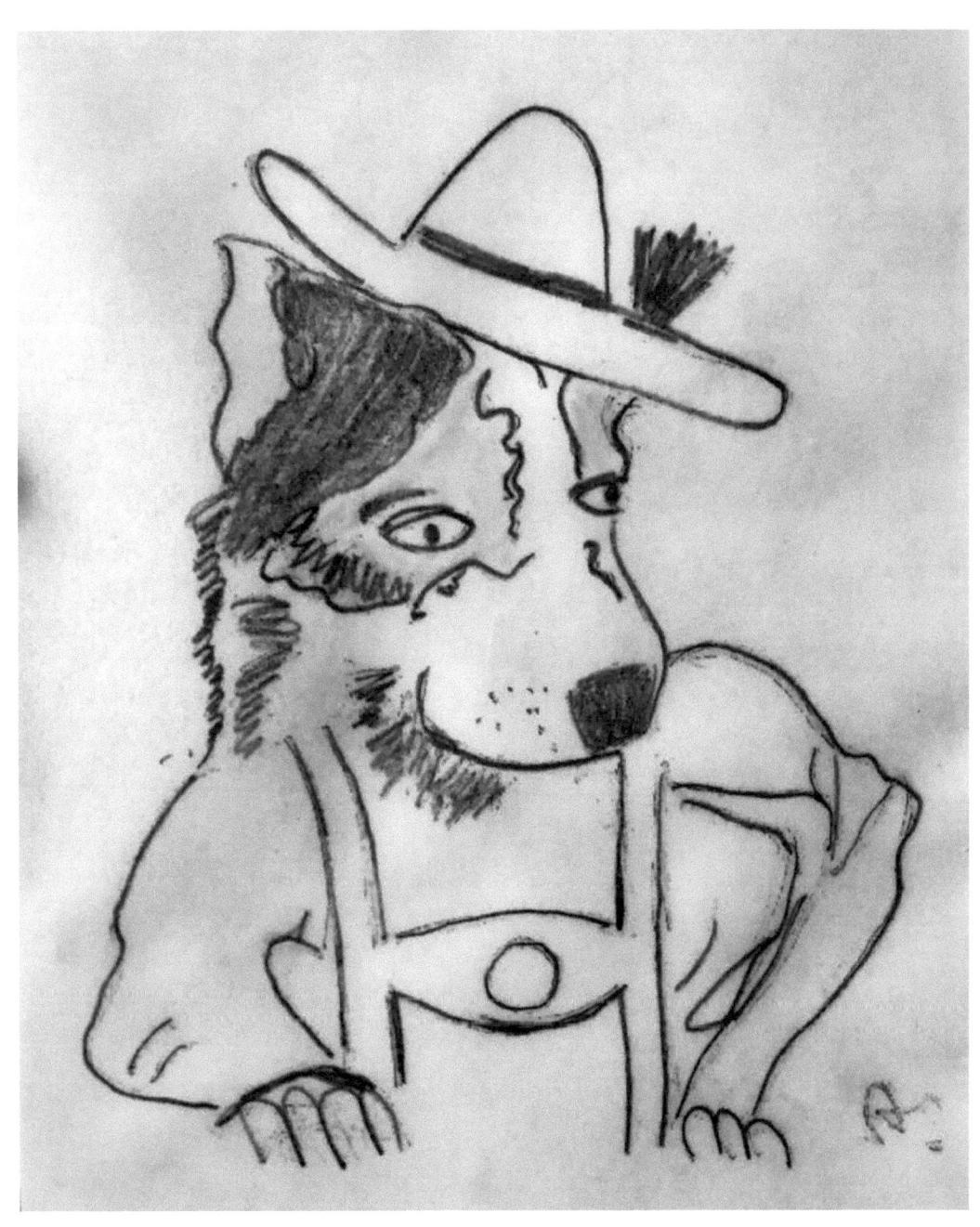

„Jodl" (Charcoal on paper)

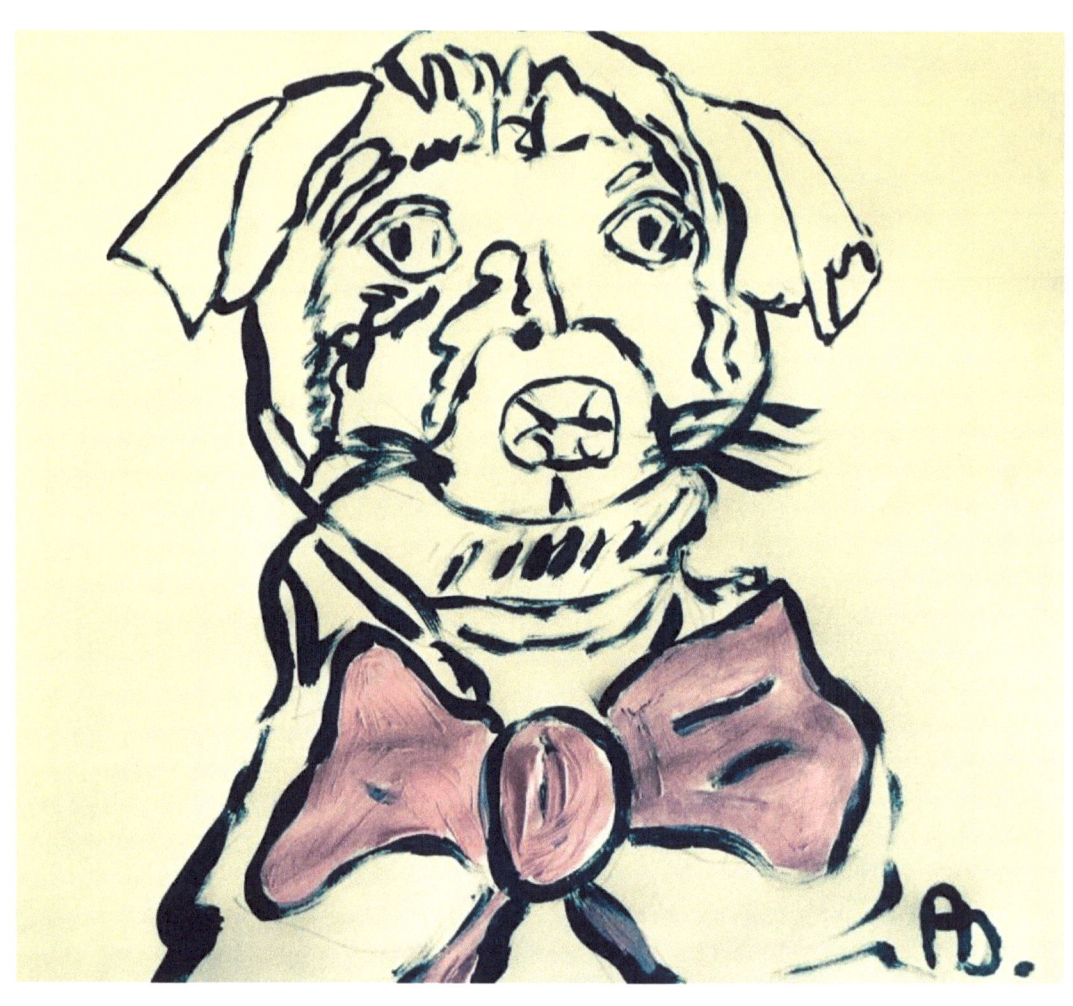

„Miss Frida" (Aquarell)

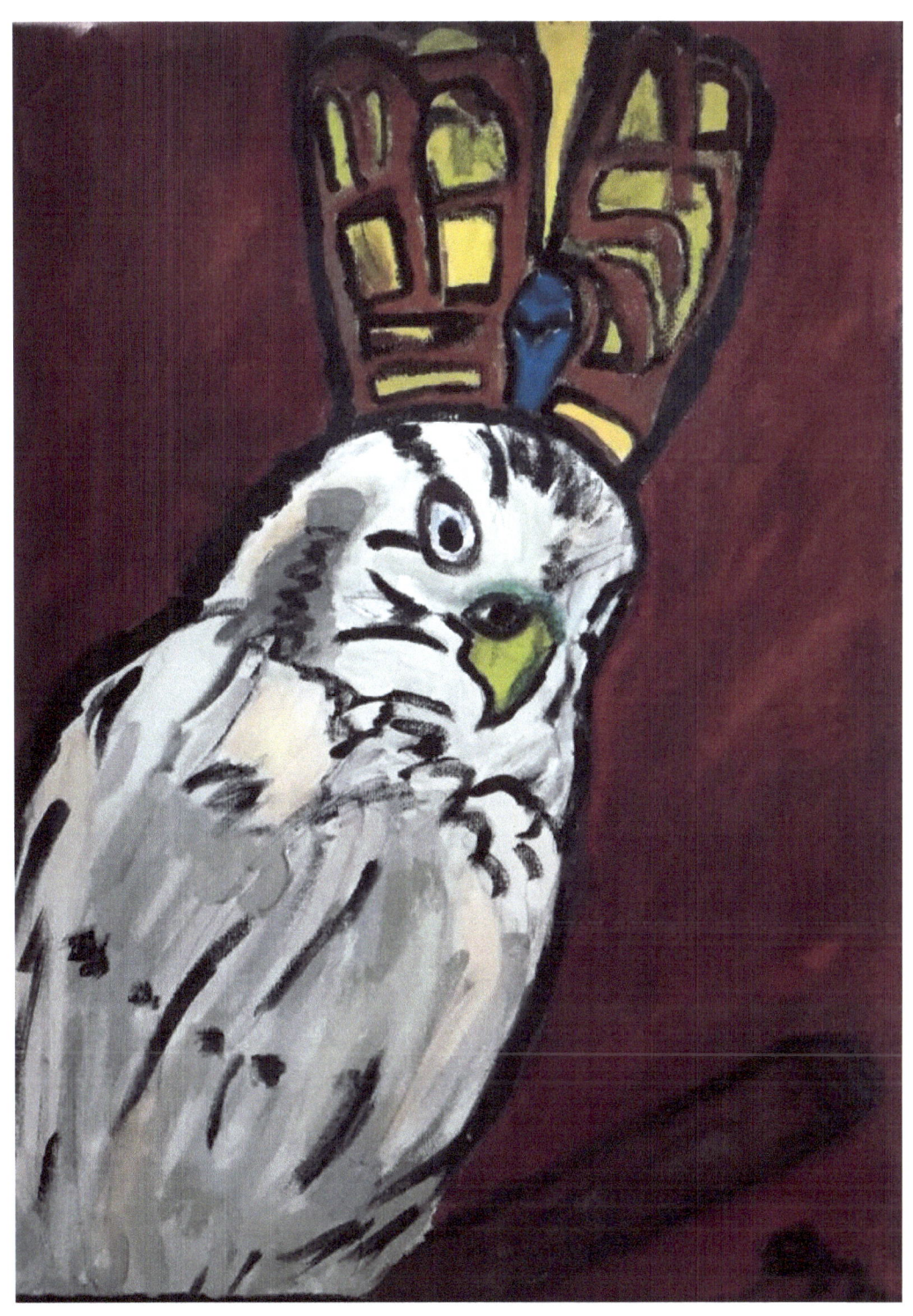

„Horus King" (Acryl on canvas)

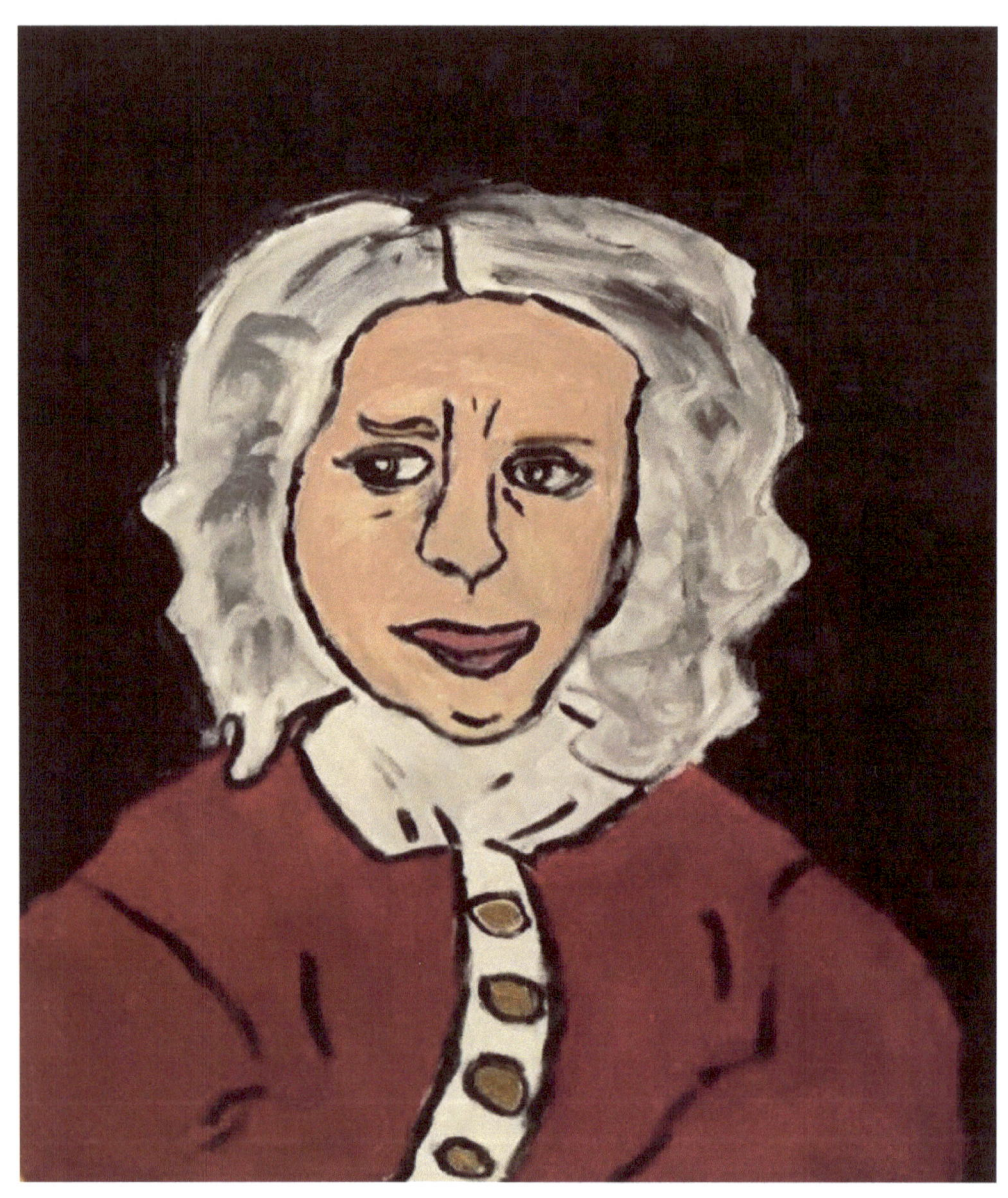

„The Count of Saint Germain" (Acryl on canvas)

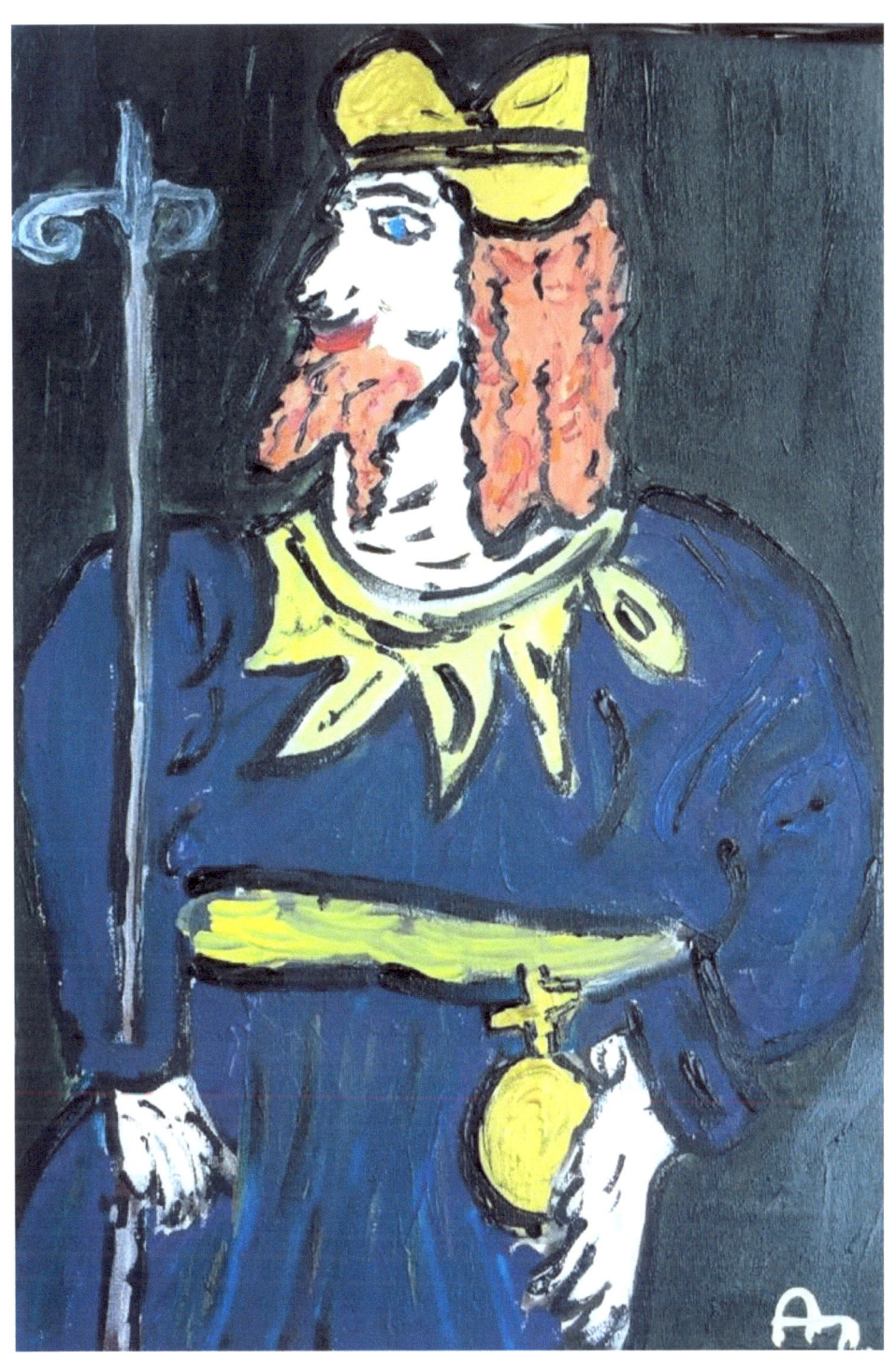

„Norman King" (Oil on canvas)

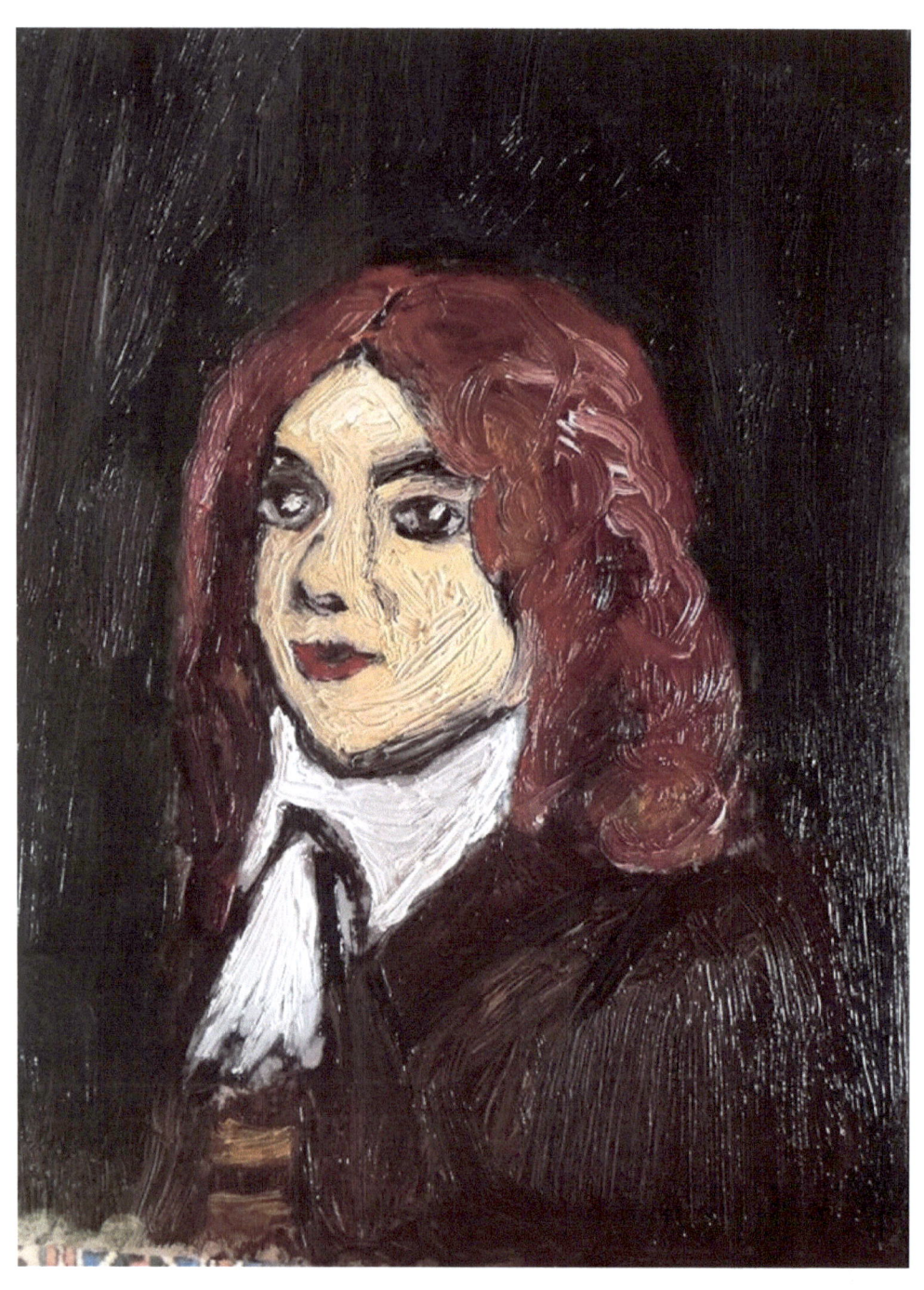

„Little Wettin boy" (Oil on canvas)

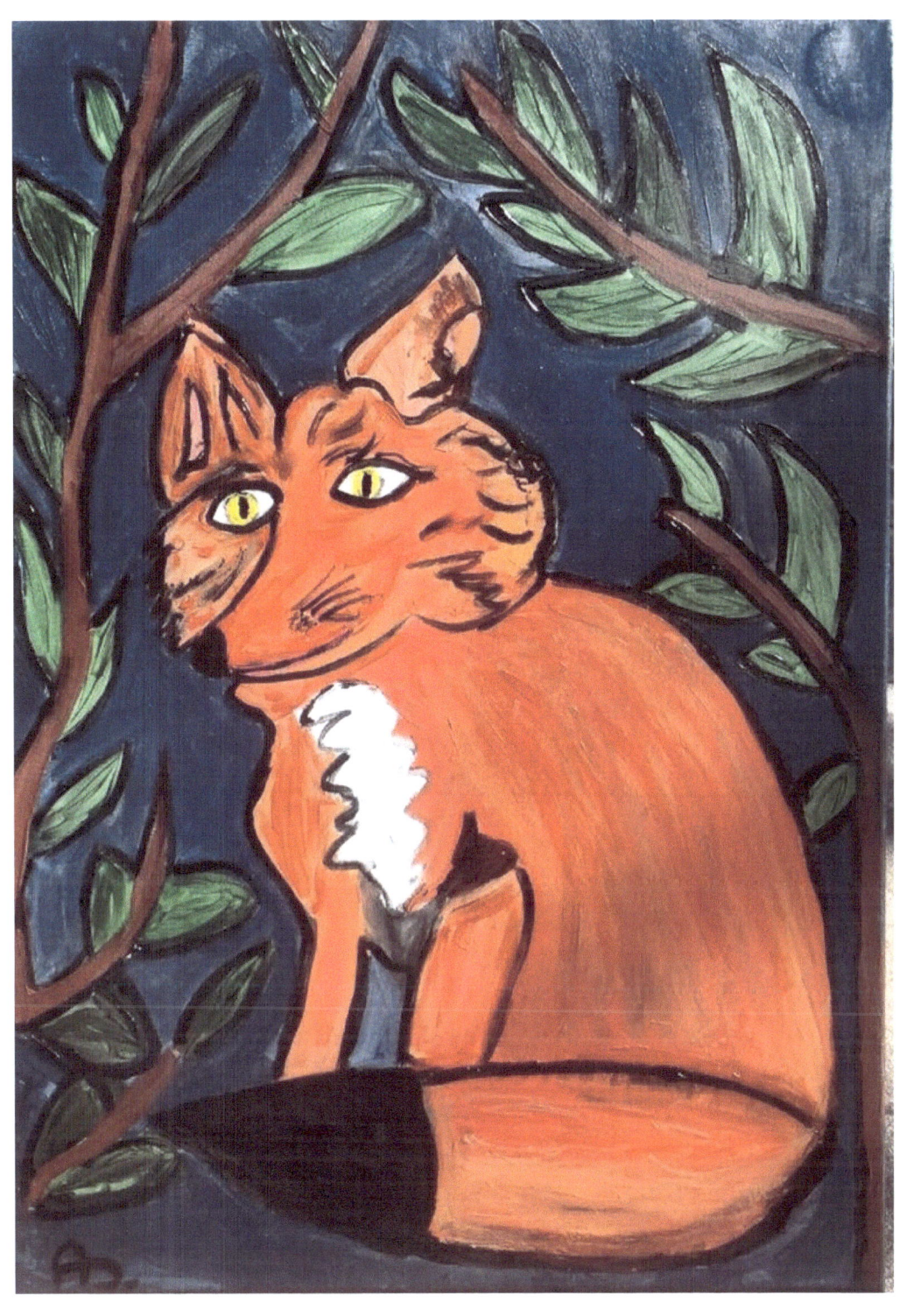

„Fox" (Acryl on canvas)

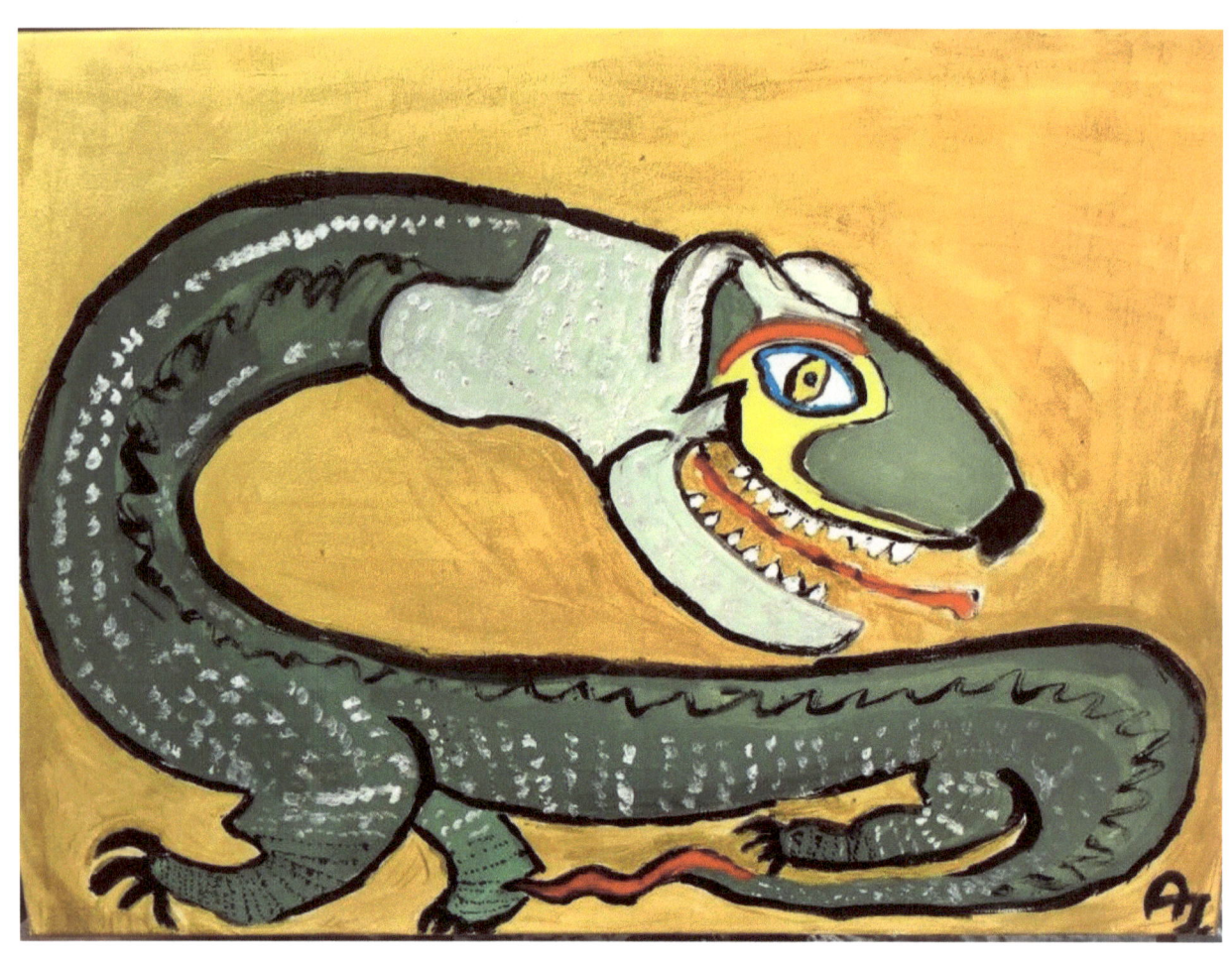

„Dragon" (Acryl on canvas)

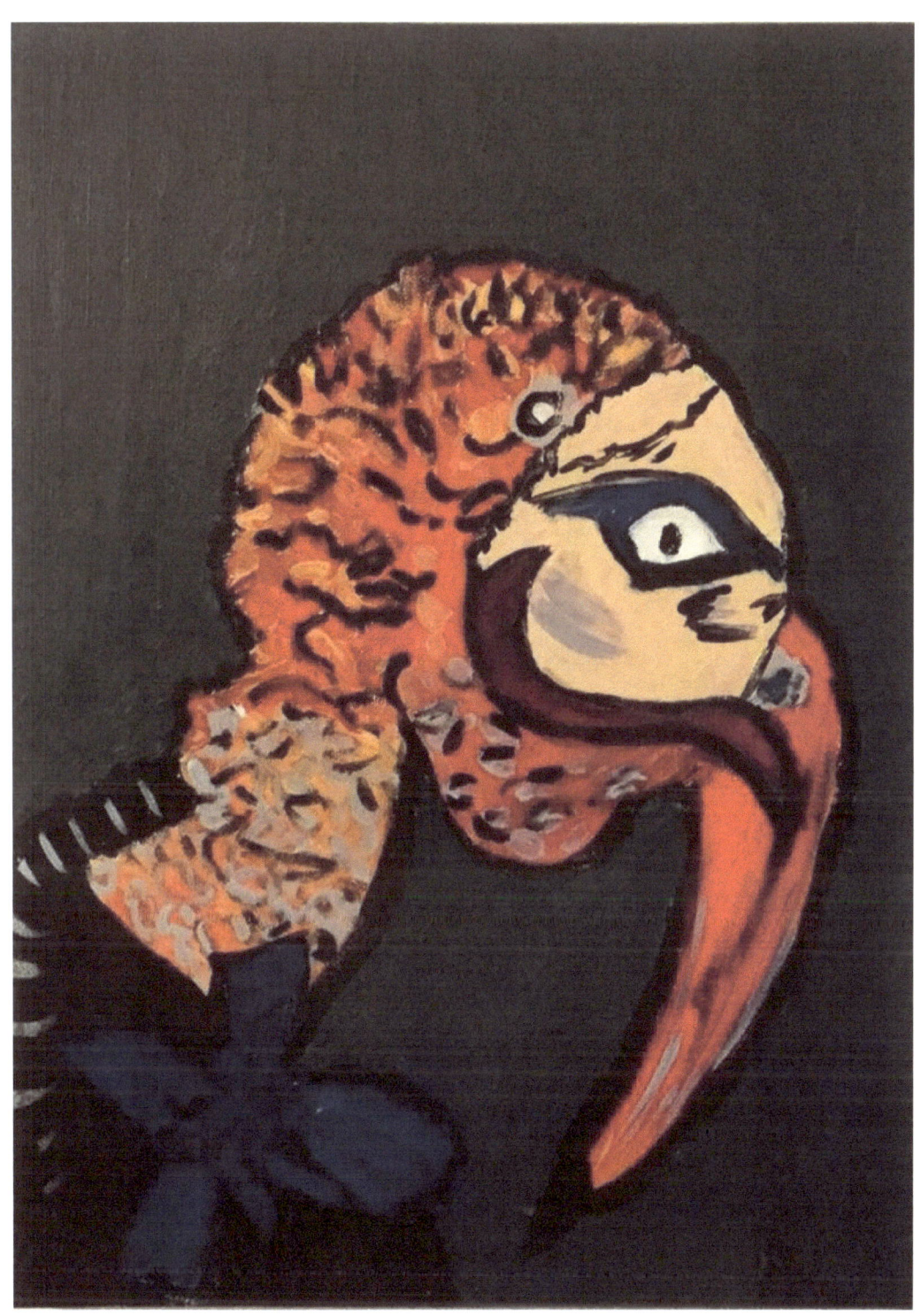

„Pilot Turkey" (Acryl on canvas)

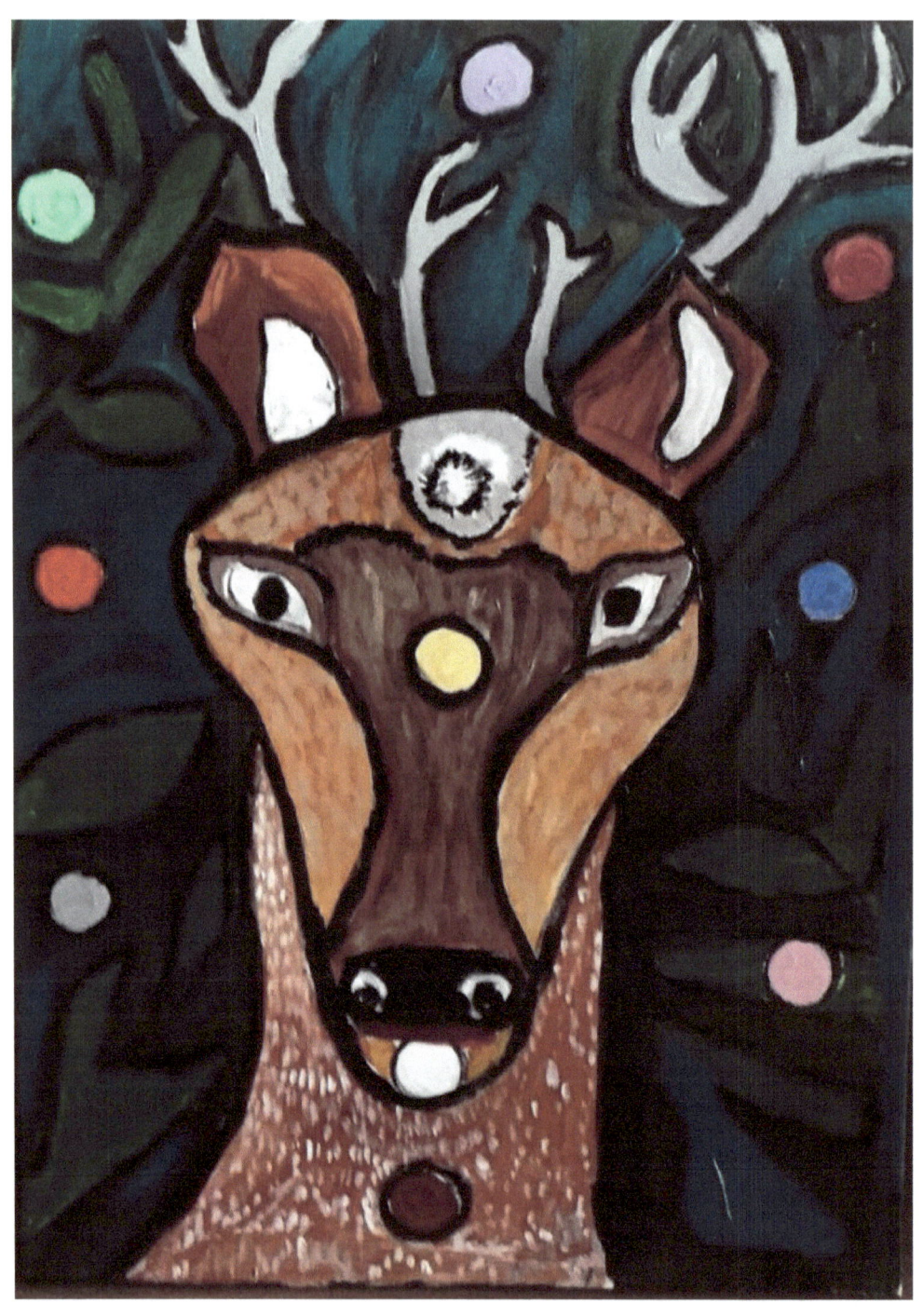

„The Tree of Life" (Acryl on canvas)

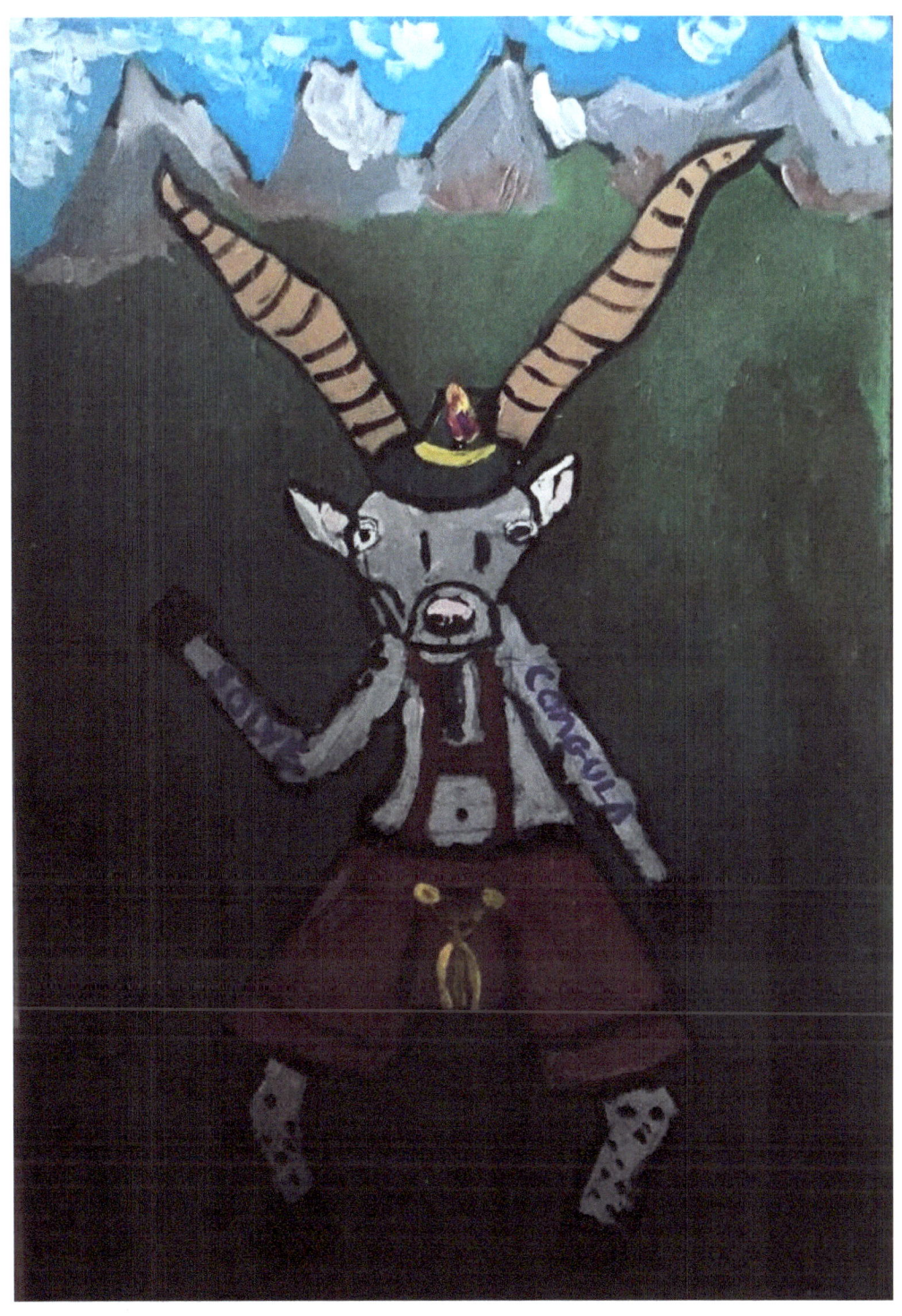

„Baphomet Bavariae (Acryl on canvas)

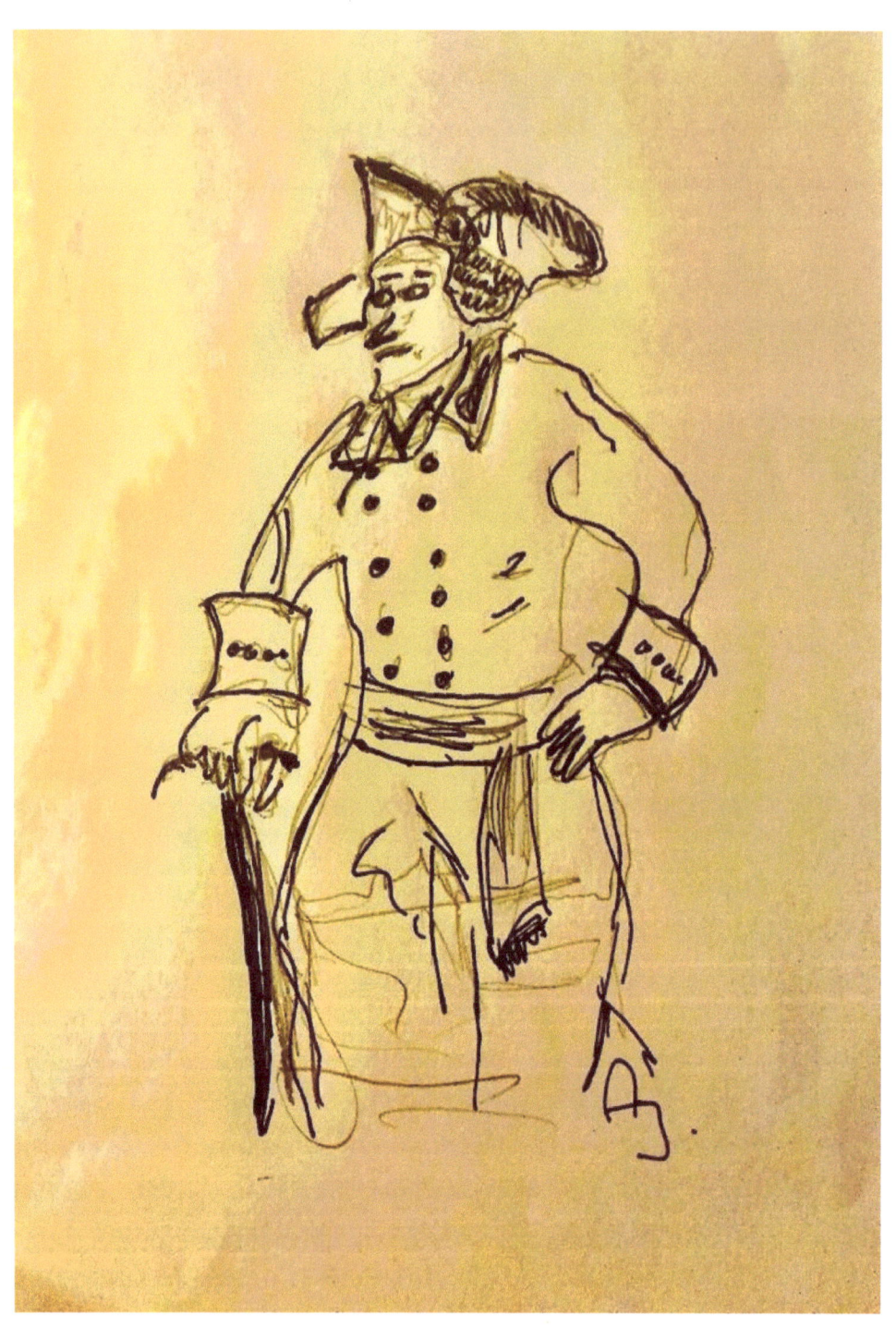

„Frederick of Prussia" (Mixed on paper)

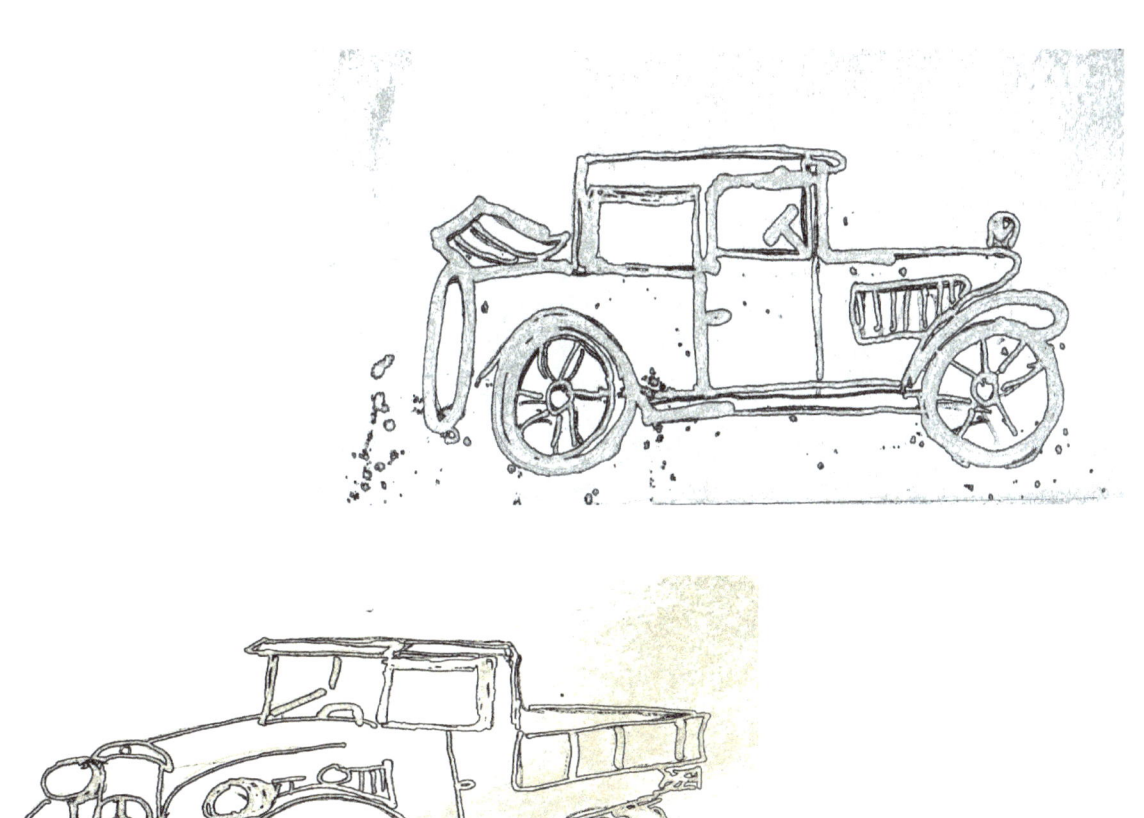

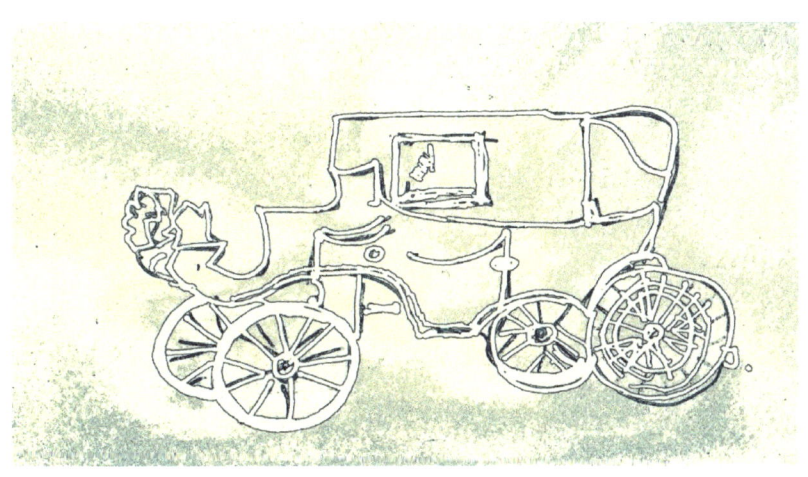

„Cars" (Mixed on paper)

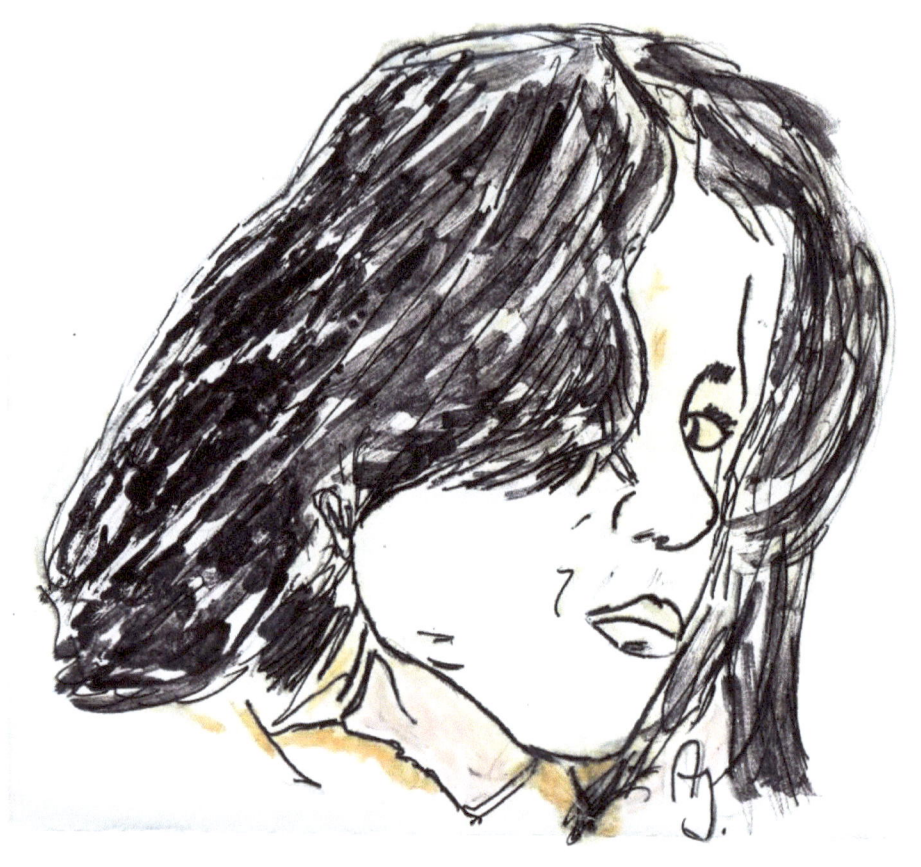

„Anja by Anja" (Mixed on paper)

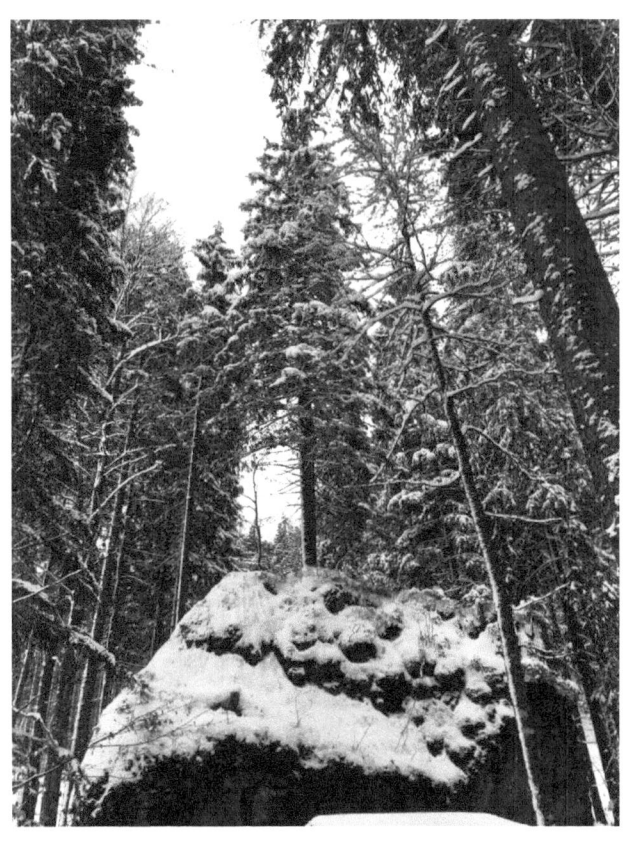

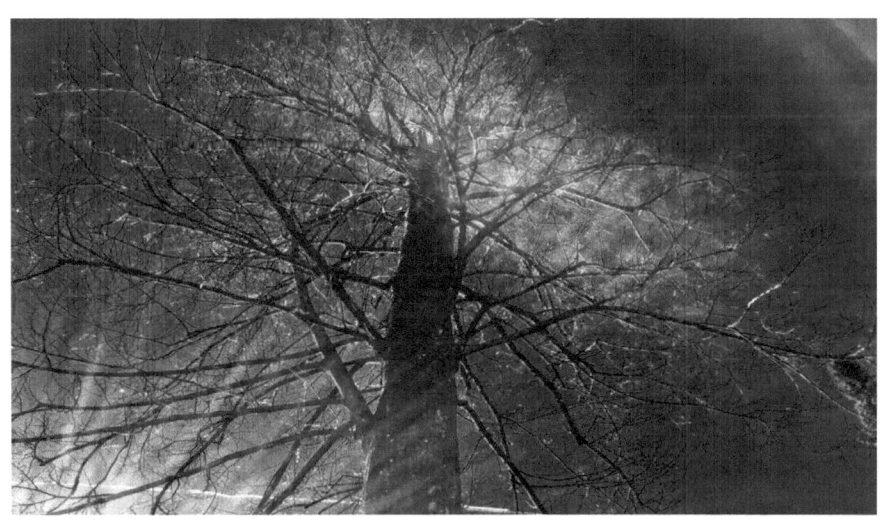

„Trees" (Photography)

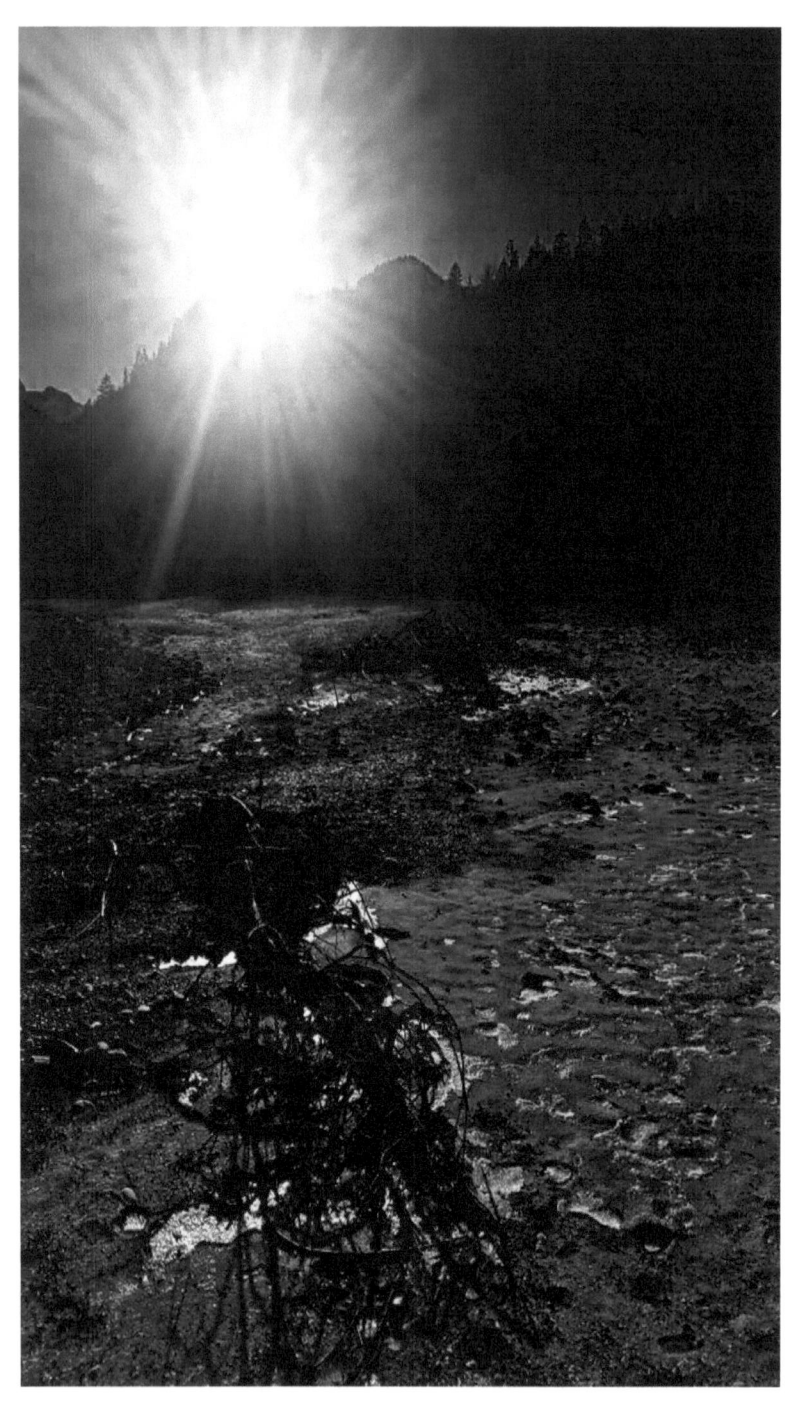

„Drought" (Photography)

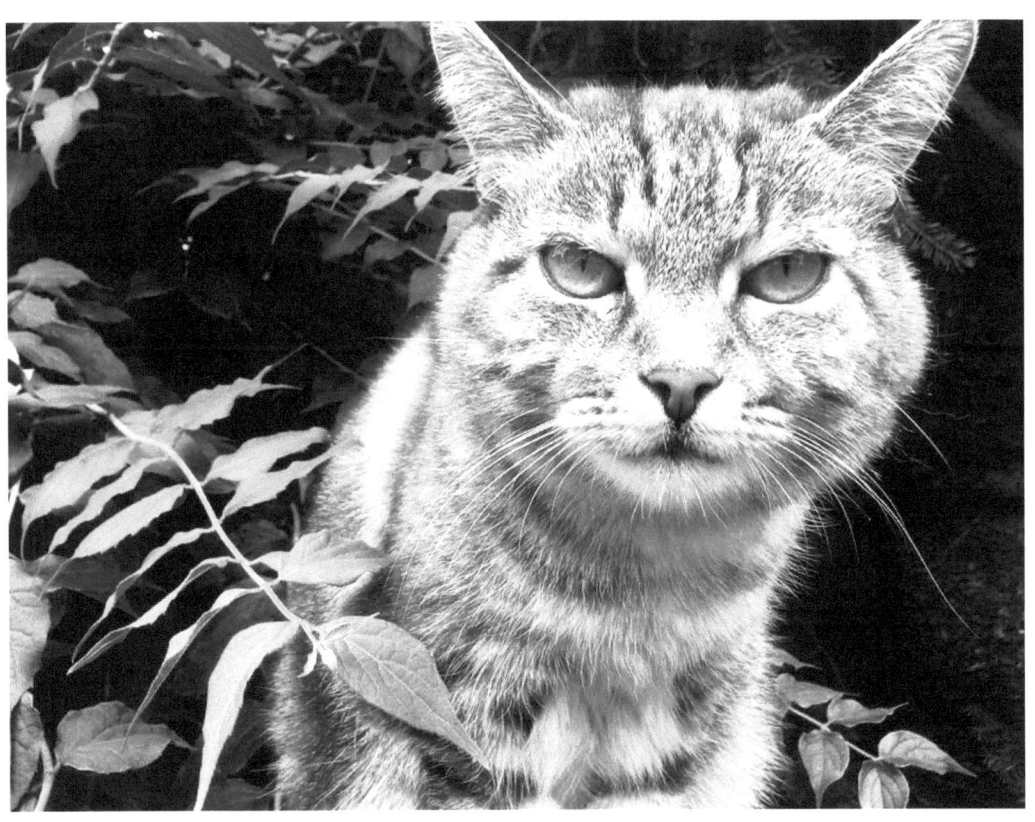

„Cat" (Photography)